The Complete Book of
Boondock RVing

Camping Off the Beaten Path

Bill and Jan Moeller

Ragged Mountain Press / McGraw-Hill

Camden, Maine ✳ New York ✳ Chicago ✳ San Francisco
✳ Lisbon ✳ London ✳ Madrid ✳ Mexico City ✳ Milan ✳
New Delhi ✳ San Juan ✳ Seoul ✳ Singapore
✳ Sydney ✳ Toronto

(RVIA)

For Jan

The McGraw·Hill Companies

1 2 3 4 5 6 7 8 9   DOC DOC   0 9 8 7

Library of Congress Cataloging-in-Publication Data
Moeller, Bill, 1930–
  The complete book of boondock RVing : camping off the beaten path / Bill Moeller.
     p.   cm.
  Includes index.
  ISBN 978-0-07-149065-8 (pbk. : alk. paper)
  1. Recreational vehicle camping—United States. I. Title.
  GV198.6M64 2007
  796.7'9—dc22   2007002812

ISBN 978-0-07-149065-8
MHID 0-07-149065-5

Questions regarding the content of this book should be addressed to
Ragged Mountain Press
P.O. Box 220
Camden, ME 04843
www.raggedmountainpress.com

Questions regarding the ordering of this book should be addressed to
The McGraw-Hill Companies
Customer Service Department
P.O. Box 547
Blacklick, OH 43004
Retail customers: 1-800-262-4729
Bookstores: 1-800-722-4726

Photographs and illustrations courtesy the author unless otherwise noted.

Contents

(RVIA)

(RVIA)

(RVIA)

Acknowledgments

We wish to thank the following people and companies for their help and support during the writing of this book: Chuck Campbell, RVing writer and photographer; Ben and Barbara Bachman of Bachman Enterprises for their TurboKOOL photos and charts; Chad Christ of East Penn Manufacturing Company, maker of Deka batteries; Miriam Robbins of Southwest Windpower for the wind generator photo; Gary Baxter and Tony Boatwright of Magnum Energy, maker of pure-sine-wave inverters; Rich Zinzer of Northwood Manufacturing for a good selection of photographs of its Nash and Arctic Fox trailers; Pamela Gray-Hann of the National Renewable Energy Laboratory for the great map of solar brightness in the United States; Daren Hatfield of Iota Engineering, maker of smart battery chargers; Stan Hackathorn of Wrangler NW Power Products for his help with high-powered alternators; Dave Needham of Progressive Dynamics, makers of fine RV products including converters; Sharon Halcomb of West Marine and Steven E. Paley of Navimo USA for the picture of Navimo flexible water tanks; and Bob Neudecker and Denis Pichii of Xantrex Technology, for pictures of several of their products. We also wish to acknowledge Greg and Deb Holder of AM Solar for working with us and adding to our knowledge of solar power. They are truly two good friends.

We also wish to thank two more very dear friends, Bob and Lynne Livingston, who have encouraged us in our writings, photography, and RVing. Bob is the man who knows the answers to all RVing problems. Thank you for being such good friends, and for having such a great sense of humor.

Lastly, I would like to thank my late wife, Jan, who was a superb writer, photographer, and traveling companion. I am giving her half of the authorship of this book even though she couldn't contribute to the work because of her illness. She did, however, encourage me to finish the book. Back some thirty years ago, when we wrote our first book, she did 95% of the work, but very generously gave me half the credit. She was a wonderful lady.

CHAPTER 1

What Is Boondock RVing?

Webster's New World Compact Desk Dictionary defines *boondocks* as "a jungle; the back-country; or a hinterland." As Jan and I understand it, the word derives from the Tagalog word for mountain—*bundok*—and was picked up by U.S. soldiers after the Spanish–American War when they were sent into the jungles of the Philippines. It became more popular during the Vietnam War and has been used more and more by the general public ever since.

Boondock RVing (or camping) is, by an RVer's definition, camping with your RV in a place where there are no electrical hookups, water faucets, sewer drains, and phone or cable TV connections. This is also called *dry camping* or *primitive camping. Boondocking RVers* are people who have their RVs equipped for this type of camping.

We first started boondocking in the 1960s, and during that time, we had two different RVs. Our first rig was a rented pickup camper, which we took on a grand tour of most of the western states. It had minimal equipment aboard: an icebox, two 110-volt lights, a two-burner

(RVIA)

1

propane cookstove, a water tank with a hand pump at the galley sink, a Humphrey propane mantle light, and a chemical toilet, which was just a large wooden box with a seat and cover, filled partly with water and chemicals to control the smell.

The trip was boondocking at its best. Our home was always with us, and we were able to pull off the road whenever we chose to eat, sleep, and rest. Camping life was simple then—and delightful. At night we would park our camper in a forest campground. With a gas light hissing away, we had comfortable warmth with plenty of light for reading and a battery-powered, shortwave radio for entertainment. The only problem we ever encountered was the lack of a furnace or heater, which we keenly felt when an early September snowstorm in Yellowstone Park left behind 6 inches of snow.

After that trip, we bought a small Tow-Low trailer, which was a big improvement. Among other things, it had an AC/propane refrigerator, a convection furnace (although no fan), a pressure water system (using a hand pump to pump up the air pressure in the water tank), and a Porta-Potti toilet. With this RV, we traveled from New York to Nebraska, up through Canada, then into New England and down the coast to our home in Connecticut, enjoying boondock camping wherever we could find it.

Today's RVs are much different from our early rigs. All the appliances and electronics in modern RVs make them seem more like houses than vehicles, what with washing machines, dishwashers, slideouts, and the like. But with the right equipment and some thoughtful planning, you can still take off in these modern RVs and enjoy the wilderness.

WHY BOONDOCK?

Ask any number of boondockers why they boondock and you'll probably get as many different answers. For example:

- Enjoy the freedom.
- Save money.
- Experience primitive camping.
- Camp in our national parks and Forest Service campgrounds.
- Convenience.
- Visit the grandkids and other relatives and be able to park in their driveway.
- Get away from it all—cell phones, PDAs, faxes, e-mails, meetings, computers, and modern life in general—as much (or as little) as you want to; these days it's easy to stay "connected" on the road.

Fun and Freedom

First and foremost, boondocking is fun. Imagine camping by a backwoods stream and having the option of either watching a football game on your satellite TV system or doing some fishing in the stream. Or you wake up with the early morning sun pushing through dense forest leaves, step out the door of your RV and onto a hiking trail. A few hours later, you come back, turn on the coffeemaker, and e-mail your Aunt Tillie all about your morning.

With boondocking, you get to enjoy freedom of choice because you're not locked into camping in a full-hookup campground. You can choose a private campground as well as a place off the beaten path. You can live simply and rough it, or pile as many amenities into your RV as you can.

We've roughed it and enjoyed it tremendously. But we also occasionally missed some of our favorite television shows, particularly football games. So we eventually got a small, black-and-white, 12-volt DC TV with a good AM/FM radio. And with our shortwave radio, we could still listen to the BBC from London, the Voice of America, or even the Voice of the Andes even if we were really in the boonies. These gave us immeasurable pleasure. Today a satellite dish operated from an inverter does the job, giving us plenty of movies, news, and sporting events to watch.

We believe it's all worth it because many of these modern conveniences make for happier camping. Boondock camping is all about being able to do what you want, when you want. Some of our books, at least in part, have been written in the comfort of our fifth-wheel trailer while we boondocked. And we've enjoyed every minute of it.

Save Money

If the main reason for boondock camping is to enjoy the experience, the second main reason is cost. RVing is one of the least expensive ways to live or travel. Many fulltimers living on fixed incomes from Social Security or pensions have found this to be true, as have families who take vacations or spend weekends camping in their RVs. Boondock camping is a wonderful way to make this experience even more affordable.

Additionally, the cost of staying in private campgrounds is increasing, going up by a dollar or more per night each year. We recently read an article in *RVBusiness* magazine, written by a campground spokesman, that stated the industry envisions campground prices will eventually reach a level of 50% of the cost of a midlevel hotel or motel. Consequently, if you would normally pay $100 a night for a hotel room, you would pay $50 a night in an RV park. Even those RVers who can afford those prices may appreciate being able to average out the yearly campground fees by boondocking as much as possible. If you pay $50 for one night's camping and then boondock for the next three nights at no cost, you have reduced your average cost to only $12.50 a night for four nights of camping.

Please understand we are not advocating ripping someone off by free camping. We have seen some RVers sneak into a private campground after the office was closed, fill their water tank, dump their sewage, leave their garbage, use the electricity, and spend the night, then leave early in the morning before the owner or manager arrives. To us this is stealing pure and simple. As you'll see in Chapter 2, there are many places where you can camp for free without cheating or stealing.

Fuel Costs

In these days of high prices for gasoline and diesel fuel, doing a little boondock camping can help equalize your RVing expenses. RVers are worried about the high fuel costs and justifiably so. On a recent solo trip with our fifth-wheel trailer from Ventura, California, to Billings, Montana, and then to Albany, Oregon, Bill spent $1,035 for fuel: 326.9 gallons of diesel fuel at an average cost of $3.15 per gallon. (Our usual mileage while towing is about 10 miles per gallon.) Bill also spent $743 for campground fees and boondocked for six nights. So figuring $25 per night, Bill saved about $150. It would have been even nicer to have boondocked throughout the whole trip. It's possible that fuel prices may come down . . . but they may also keep going up. In any event, saving $150 is always a good thing!

A recent Recreation Vehicle Industry Association (RVIA) news release poll discussed this issue of fuel costs in light of RVing trends. Some of the results are listed below:

- 45% of RV owners said they may stay closer to home for their camping than they have in the past.

- 52% said they will stay a week or longer at one site to save on fuel costs.

- 67% said they will still use their RVs more than in the previous year.

- 37% reported that the cost of fuel would not affect their RV travel plans.

So whether you alter your RVing habits by traveling less or make no changes at all, you still can benefit from boondocking.

Experience Nature

There are many good reasons for staying in private campgrounds. You can enjoy the convenience of electrical hookups, cable TV, laundry facilities, a sewer dump at the site, and free running water. And there are times when a private campground is a necessity. In fact, we stay in them the majority of the time, particularly when we have a writing project to do or when we are in a hurry to get to a certain place.

But there are other times when we feel the need to get out in the wild and feed our psyches by being free. And being free means camping in an out-of-the-way place, so we can smell the mountain air, hear the waves crashing on an ocean beach, or enjoy a scenic view. The wilderness is our particular religion, our place of worship, our nourishment.

Sometimes the wilderness is just an adventure in the unexpected, such as the time in Waterton Lakes National Park in Canada when a bull elk looking for his bride decided to bugle 20 feet away from our trailer at 2:30 in the morning. It got our attention real fast, but it has also given us something to talk about ever since.

While some people may see boondocking as a means to beat the high cost of private camping, we believe most RVers think of it as a way to be close to the environment in a natural setting. Falling asleep at night listening to an owl hooting near your rig or waking up in a beautiful location, perhaps close to special activities you like—such experiences are part of the joys of boondocking.

We are fortunate to live in a country that offers so many places to get close to nature, such as our national parks and forests and recreation areas, all of which have boondocking campsites (see Chapter 2). Most small state and county parks are also dry camps. A few may have electricity available, but that is all, and it will most likely be an old 15 amp outlet. Some dry camps might even have a trash station, but in effect you are still boondocking. A lot of the parks in the mountains or along our beaches have nothing more than a space in which to park your rig.

RVers boondocking on the beach at Seward, Alaska.

Convenience

Overnight convenience camping is when an RVer pulls into the parking lot of a shopping center, restaurant, or retail store for one night, strictly for convenience's sake, and resumes traveling the next day. Most RVers do it, at least occasionally, and we have frequently done this type of boondock camping. Sometimes an area has no nearby campgrounds or the local campgrounds are full, or we are just trying to save a bit of money. Any modern RV is usually equipped for overnight convenience camping, and if you're careful to conserve your battery power, you'll have no problems.

This topic, in fact, was discussed in an article in the July/August 2006 issue of *Escapees* magazine, the official publication of the Escapees RV Club, which promotes boondock camping. The article, "An Economist's Perspective," was written by Andrew Cornwall, who did a study for the government of Nova Scotia, Canada. The study investigated the economic effects on private campgrounds of a province-wide, overnight RV parking ban in business parking lots. The study's results apply to RVers in both Canada and the United States:

- Half of all RVers boondock in such parking lots.

- RVers stay in these lots 1.5 nights per month for each month they use their RVs, plus 0.6 night for each 1,000 miles traveled.

- Convenience was the overwhelming reason given, followed by the lack of available camping sites in the area.

- The existence of a parking ban caused one third of all RVers to boycott an area and one half to have a diminished desire to visit the area.

These results demonstrate that all RVers need to boondock occasionally, and that more and more RVers are boondocking.

Another aspect of convenience camping is being able to visit friends and family and park your RV in their driveway or backyard. You have the privacy and peace of mind of separate living quarters, yet the convenience of being able to walk across the yard to have breakfast with your grandchildren. Or you're in the reverse situation—you and your children are the ones visiting Mom and Dad. Since your RV is already stocked and prepared for children, your visit is that much more relaxed and organized.

EXTENDED BOONDOCK CAMPING

Extended camping is when an RVer plans to stay at a site for two nights or more, perhaps even a week, a month, or a full season. This type of camping requires some specialized knowledge, equipment, and techniques to do it successfully. These are primarily electrical in nature, with the most important concern being the proper charging of your battery. (We'll cover the electrical aspects of boondocking in the latter part of the book.)

The reasons for this type of boondock camping also vary:

- Enjoy the wilderness or the away-from-it-all experience.

- Fish the rivers and streams of a particular area.

- Provide a base camp for hunting, rock climbing, hiking, skiing, or snowmobiling.

Many snowbirds go to the desert areas of the Southwest and stay for a month or even the entire season, camping without benefit of hookups. The most popular place for boondocking is the stretch of highway between Yuma and the popular center of all boondock camping—Quartzsite, Arizona. Quartzsite's population increases every January, February, and March from 2,000 people to over 500,000 RVers and rockhounds for the RV and Gem Shows held during this period. Once at Quartzsite, we met a lady who told us she had lived there for seven years without any hookups of any kind. Now that is really boondocking!

A SAMPLE BOONDOCKING TRIP

To give you an idea of what boondocking might be like, we've created the following fictional, but typical, trip. We'll follow Bob and Mary Jones as they take a two-week boondock camping trip. Their RV is a 30-foot Class A motorhome (see Chapter 3 for more on types of RVs), and they tow a vehicle (which RVers call a dinghy). As you read, please don't let the technical talk bother you; we've included cross-references to direct you to the main discussions in the book.

Many RVers camping at Quartzsite, Arizona, the mecca of boondock camping.

First let's look at the equipment installed in Bob and Mary's RV:

■ A converter/charger with a 45 amp output.

■ A 4-kilowatt built-in generator. (Trailers can have this same convenience with a small portable generator of at least 1,000 watts.)

■ A 300-watt portable inverter wired to the batteries.

■ Two 100-watt solar panels with a multistage regulator featuring maximum power point tracking (MPPT).

■ Two 6-volt golf-cart wet-cell batteries, wired in series, with a total capacity of 220 amp-hours.

■ A 30-watt TV satellite receiver (runs off the inverter).

■ A 9-inch, 35-watt color TV set (runs off the inverter).

■ A 17-inch, wide-screen, 75-watt laptop computer with a 120-volt AC power supply (runs off the inverter).

■ A standard 12-volt DC/120-volt AC propane refrigerator.

■ A cell phone.

■ A SmoothTalker cell-phone amplifier.

■ An engine alternator capable of delivering at least a 30 amp charge.

■ A 50-gallon freshwater tank.

■ Two 6-gallon jerry jugs for extra fresh water.

■ Holding tanks: a 36-gallon gray-water tank and a 36-gallon black-water tank.

■ Two 7-gallon propane tanks.

Day 1

Our couple, Bob and Mary, leave home for a two-week vacation. They spend their first day driving along the interstate highway to their first night's destination—a convenience boondock stop in a Wal-Mart parking lot (see Chapter 2). They arrive late in the afternoon, put the refrigerator on propane, and do a little shopping.

In the evening, they extend their slideouts (sections of an RV that extend about 2 to 4 feet beyond the normal width of the unit), and using the inverter, spend a few hours watching satellite TV. They also have the option of answering their e-mail on the laptop by using a cell-phone PC card and amplifier (see Chapter 7). Bob decides to surf the Internet for awhile looking for places to go.

With all this electricity usage, they will closely monitor their batteries' amp-hour consumption tonight using one of the following instruments: an ammeter, an amp-hour meter (best choice), or a volt-ohm meter (VOM; see Chapter 9). They could also go low-tech and just estimate their evening's amp-hour consumption (see Table 8-3).

Day 2

Our couple decides to get an early start this morning. Since they plan to drive several hundred miles today, they're confident the alternator will charge the batteries enough to replenish the previous night's discharge (see Chapter 10). If not, they can use the solar panels in conjunction with the alternator to do the job (see Chapter 12). Another option would be to charge the batteries using the generator and the converter/charger as they travel throughout the day (see Chapter 11).

Bob and Mary finally arrive at their destination, which is the first wilderness camping site they plan to visit. As they have previously visited the site before, they know exactly where they wish to park their RV—along a pretty mountain river. After setting up their camp, they drive to nearby Bureau of Land Management (BLM) or Forest Service offices to pick up some maps of the region and generally explore the area (see Chapter 2).

So far today, the only electrical appliance in use is the refrigerator. (Note: We never travel with the refrigerator in the On position. This not only conserves electrical power and propane, but more important, avoids the danger of a propane explosion or fire in the event of a highway accident; see Chapter 5.) Because it's a hot day, Bob will be sure to run the refrigerator for an hour or so when they stop for lunch. If they keep the doors closed, this should be enough time to keep the food cool until they reach their campsite. The refrigerator is the highest phantom load in the RV (see Chapter 8). It can consume up to 1 ampere per hour or 24 amp-hours per day.

Tonight Bob and Mary discuss whether to prepare their evening meal in the galley or cook it outside over a small outdoor grill that they carry with them (see Chapter 5). Later they hope to build a fire in a clear area near their RV and invite neighbors over for a visit. Many a friendship has begun sitting around a crackling fire, telling camping stories. In addition, they can save a lot of amp-hours of battery power while having loads of fun in the process. However, if Bob and Mary repeat the previous night's entertainment, they will need to keep the amp-hour consumption down so they won't have a lot of charging to do the next day.

Day 3

Today is the first day that Bob and Mary may have to do some serious battery charging. The solar panels will do the job for them, providing they've situated the RV on the site to give the panels the maximum sunlight from a southerly direction. The panels can be tilted so the sun's rays are perpendicular to the surface of the solar panels, but most RVers don't bother to do this except in the winter when the sun is low in the sky. Solar panels can be the best way to charge the batteries as long as their installation has been planned around the RV's power needs. When this is done properly, charging is automatic and quiet.

Next the couple either checks the amp-hour meter or calculates last night's battery discharge (see Chapter 8). This will give them an idea of how long it will take to restore the batteries to full power. They turn on the solar panels when they get up to catch the early morning rays. If the day is sunny, they should see a small charge almost immediately, and by nine o'clock, 1 to 2 amps or more. Checking to make sure that all electrical items are turned off, except the fridge, Mary and Bob leave to explore a primitive mountain road that looked interesting on the map. As they drive, the road eventually peters out, so they hike up the trace for a mile or so with their cameras, seeing several deer and a bull elk on the way.

When Bob and Mary return to the RV, the batteries are fully charged. After supper, they watch a DVD movie on their wide-screen computer. Other amp-hour usage will be the refrigerator and room lights (12-volt lights) for a total of about 12 amp-hours for the evening.

Day 4

The morning dawns with a heavy cloud cover, so the solar panels are hardly charging at all. Happily, the meters (or calculations) show that the batteries are only slightly discharged, perhaps to a level of around 36 amp-hours (see Chapter 9). Bob and Mary decide to "leave it up to the sun" for the charging. This morning they plan to check out the fish in the river. After several hours of fishing, they've caught two nice trout, big enough for supper. By early afternoon, the sun has burned off the clouds so the panels have kicked in and are now charging the batteries.

Now that they've reached their fourth day, Bob and Mary must start to consider the amount of water in the freshwater tank and the levels of the gray- and black-water holding tanks (see Chapter 4). They can easily extend their freshwater supply by filling up their 6-gallon jerry jugs. The holding tanks, however, are a different matter. Once they are full, the couple will have to break camp to empty them. (Many longtime boondockers carry an auxiliary tank for emptying their holding tank; however, Bob and Mary have always viewed that option as being a lot of extra work for little gain.)

Our couple spends the evening watching the news and doing a little computer work.

Day 5

Bob decides that since they have no neighbors to disturb, he's going to try out his generator for charging the batteries (see Chapter 11). As he has a good converter/charger with a 45 amp rating, he wants to see how long it will take to get the job done. Mary's plan is to finish the book she has been reading, then maybe start another. So she takes a folding camp chair down to the stream, along with a cup of coffee and her book.

Only a little more than 2 hours later, Bob is surprised and pleased to find the batteries are already fully charged according to the amp-hour meter.

After lunch, Bob and Mary drive to a small town nearby for groceries, including two fine steaks to cook on the grill for dinner that night. After dinner, they play a little gin rummy, with Mary winning twice. Bob warns he will win at hearts the next time they play. Because they played cards, their only battery consumption tonight is a single 12-volt lamp and the ever-present refrigerator. This is a good way to boondock occasionally to conserve battery power.

Day 6

Today will be another travel day. Since the batteries were not severely discharged during the past evening's activities, Bob figures the alternator should be able to charge them while they travel. But if necessary, they can also use the solar panels or the built-in generator while traveling. Mary reminds Bob that the holding tanks are getting full, and they need to fill the freshwater tank. They come to the conclusion that they should stay at a private campground that night so they can fully charge the batteries, empty the holding tanks (and not have to carry the hundreds of pounds of extra weight), and top off the freshwater tank. After arriving at the campground, they invite some nearby relatives to visit and see their new RV. This evening they won't have worry about power consumption because the converter/charger will keep the batteries fully charged as well as provide all the current they'll need for the refrigerator and lights.

Day 7

Today is another moving day, so our RVers hitch up their tow vehicle and drive several hundred miles to a nice state park, which has dry camping in a lovely canyon campground beneath a pretty waterfall. Here they plan to rendezvous with two other RVing friends, Joe and Vicki, who have a 29-foot fifth-wheel trailer. Our friends set up camp in a site that will let the sun reach the solar panels, but where they also can enjoy the camaraderie of their fellow RVers.

Later in the day, Bob and Mary hike into the mountains and come back in time for a big frankfurter cookout and potluck dinner at the site next to their friends, who have just arrived. Tonight everyone sits around the fire and talks for hours. All this outdoor activity helps keep the batteries charged because no high-amperage items are used except for a few cabin lights and the refrigerator.

Day 8

This morning is beautiful, so Bob, Mary, Joe, and Vicki decide to head out for a hike. Their campground is located at the end of a small mountain range that runs for 25 or 30 miles back into the wilderness. The trail they'll be following will take them up to a beautiful lake at an elevation of around 9,000 feet. They plan to hike up to the lake where they'll have lunch, then hike back down again to the campground. Mary and Vicki have a good time picking wildflowers, while Bob and Joe enjoy a trip up a side canyon where they see many deer.

They arrive back at their RVs, have a cold meal for supper, and retire early—it was a long hike.

Day 9

The day dawns dark and windy. The ladies decide they want to make it an easy day and do nothing more than sit around reading: Mary with her new book and Vicki with a good mystery she's just started.

Joe is having a problem charging his batteries with the solar panels, so Bob rigs a long extension cord from his AC onboard generator to Joe's AC converter/charger. With this setup, they can charge Joe's battery bank with Bob's generator. After a few hours, Joe's battery bank is charged, so Bob charges his own batteries. Next they take a look at Joe's solar panels and discover that the problem is nothing more than a loose wire. After a tasty sandwich lunch, and since the sun has now come out, both couples decide to climb to the top of the waterfall and take some pictures. That night they enjoy a large campfire, with some of their neighbors joining in.

Day 10

This morning Bob and Mary say good-bye to Joe and Vicki as the friends part, each going their own way. Bob and Mary want to go over to the coast and stay at a park above the beach. They have stayed at this park before, and it has electric and water services available. Although they don't need the water service, the electrical hookup will be nice for a change.

After setting up camp, Bob and Mary head out to a small, nearby city that has an "Old Town" with many interesting shops and several nice restaurants. They do some souvenir hunting, and later enjoy an excellent halibut dinner and a glass of wine. Having the luxury of electrical service, they make full use of the TV by watching Monday Night Football, during which Bob's team loses and Mary's team wins.

Day 11

Our RVers continue farther up the coast today to an excellent boondocking state park, where they plan to stay overnight. The park has a few sites on the bluffs overlooking the ocean, and Bob and Mary want to get there early. With great views and wonderful breezes, these sites fill up fast and are on a first-come, first-serve basis.

They arrive in time to find a nice site and set up camp. The day is spent doing small chores, followed by a short walk. Bob has recently acquired a wind generator, and since they are in an area with good winds, he wants to try it out (see Chapter 12). He sets up the unit on a pole fastened to a picnic table, and using Gator Clamps, he connects the charge cord to the batteries.

Immediately the generator starts charging at 6 amps as the wind is blowing between 10 and 15 miles per hour. Not bad for a charging device that will work night and day. (All these charging devices are a trade-off: you must have wind for the wind generator to work and sunlight for the solar panels.)

For dinner Mary whips up a good meal from the RV's pantry of canned goods and a few vegetables. For entertainment tonight, they find they can reach a cell-phone tower with their SmoothTalker antenna (see Chapter 7). This allows them to call the family, followed by a few hours of surfing the Web on the computer.

Day 12

Bob's first task today is to check the batteries, and he finds they are fully charged. The wind generator worked great. Next the couple prepares to get underway. One of the big pluses of boondock camping is that you have only a minimal amount of preparation to get underway in the morning. Today the couple needs to drive several hundred miles to get them closer to home. They plan to stay at a casino that is on the way (see Chapter 2).

As soon as Bob and Mary arrive at the casino, they check in with security for permission to camp overnight. (This permission is required because all casinos have very good security systems, and security staff need to know who is staying overnight. Note, however, that rules vary from casino to casino.) Having overnighted at casinos on other occasions, Bob and Mary know that they should not put out their awnings or set up the grill or lawn chairs. In the evening, though, they extend the slideouts before visiting the casino.

Inside the casino, the couple enjoys a delicious supper at the buffet, then they hit the slots. Mary wins $150, while poor Bob wins zilch.

Day 13

Today is the last full day of camping before Bob and Mary arrive home. As it will be an easy day, only about a hundred miles to drive, they decide on a late start. Their destination is a rest area with a dump station, located on a small highway (see Chapter 2). This stop will allow them to arrive home with empty holding tanks.

When they arrive at the rest area, Bob sees that all the parking is under the trees, so he won't be able to use the solar panels. He's not worried, however, because they can charge their batteries when they get home.

Day 14

Since this will be a long day of driving, Bob and Mary plan an early start. The miles glide by, and Bob and Mary arrive home in the late afternoon. Bob parks the RV in the yard and hooks up the electric cable.

As they chat that night about their trip, both agree it was a wonderful adventure. They got to spend two weeks visiting places they could not have seen or enjoyed as much if they had not been boondocking.

Although Bob and Mary's trip is pure fiction, we hope it gives you a sense of what boondock camping is like. The locations Bob and Mary camped are also fictitious, but they are similar to actual places we've visited.

Over the years, boondock camping has been some of the most enjoyable camping we've done. We hope the information in this book will encourage you to venture out and do the same.

CHAPTER 2

Where to Go Boondock RVing?

Now that you've decided you want to try your hand at boondock camping, where do you go? For starters, there are hundreds of public campgrounds all over the country in national forests and parks and on public lands. We've visited many of these campgrounds and enjoyed them tremendously. Some of our most memorable places have been the Bighorn Mountains and along the Hoback River, just south of Jackson Hole, Wyoming. But sometimes our campsite has been as simple as a rest area or a wide spot on the side of the road. A suitable site for us is anywhere that has a flat piece of land where we can set up camp for the night. In this chapter, we'll give you lots of ideas for finding your own boondock campsites.

(Winnebago Industries)

Planning Your Trip

Before you leave on a boondock adventure, some trip planning will help ensure you have a pleasurable experience. Although it's great fun to find an unexpected gem of a campground, and we encourage such wanderlust, some planning is always a good idea.

First, get as much information as you can about the campsites you plan to visit before you leave:

- What facilities are available?
- Do you need reservations?
- If you don't make reservations, is it likely that a site will be available?
- What size RVs will the roads and campsites accommodate?
- Are there any restrictions?

You can gather this and similar information from campground directories and travel guides (see the Recommended Reading appendix), park brochures, websites, and phone calls, or you might want to visit the park or campground ahead of time.

While much of the charm of boondocking is the freedom to camp when and where you please, you still have to maintain and manage your RV's resources; i.e., recharge batteries, replenish water and propane supplies, and empty holding tanks. For example, spending extended boondocking time at a site where there is so much tree cover you can't use your solar panels may mean an interim visit at a campground with electrical hookups or some travel time on the road to recharge your battery bank (see Chapter 9). Or you may find yourself running out of water and the dry camp has no freshwater source. So as you plan where you want to go, also plan for handling these tasks, especially if you are a novice boondocker.

PUBLIC BOONDOCKING SITES

Various government and state agencies manage and oversee public recreation areas, forests, and parks.

Bureau of Land Management Recreation Areas

The Bureau of Land Management (BLM) is an agency of the Department of the Interior and administers 258 million acres of public lands. Recreation areas within these public lands are often situated along good fishing streams and rivers, making them very popular with fishermen. We often stay in BLM campgrounds. In addition to the scenery, they usually have flat areas in which to park, trash cans, and pit toilets (although we always use the toilet in our RV).

To find these recreation areas, you can start with the book *Adventures on America's Public Lands*, written by BLM staffers, a full-color guidebook to BLM recreation areas. The guidebook contains maps, photos, site specifics (e.g., fees, amenities, contact information), and available activities.

Our fifth-wheel at the BLM's Bayhorse Recreation Site along the Salmon River near Challis, Idaho.

On the BLM site (www.blm.gov), clicking on the Recreation link under Programs, and then on Trip Planning will give you helpful information and links. One link is to Recreation.gov (www.recreation.gov), which has comprehensive information on recreational sites for all federal public lands, including BLM recreation areas. You can also make online reservations for certain sites.

Forest Service Campgrounds

The U.S. Forest Service (USFS), an agency of the U.S. Department of Agriculture, manages public lands in national forests and grasslands. Their campgrounds are often situated in very beautiful places and are quite popular. Select Recreational Activities from the home page of the Forest Service website, www.fs.fed.us, and you'll be able to find a forest (you can search by name or by state), request maps and brochures, get information on passes and permits, and learn about special programs and outdoor safety. The information provided for each national forest varies—some give a great deal of detailed information, others less than you might want. There will always be a way to contact someone (via phone and/or e-mail) if you have more questions.

However, national forests may have potential problems for some RVers as many of them were constructed in the 1940s and 1950s and only accommodate smaller RVs. For example:

- Many campsites are too short and narrow to accommodate slideouts.

- Roads through the grounds are often narrow and winding. Often, trees are growing at the edge of the road, making negotiating tight turns difficult or impossible.

- Branches hanging over the sites and roads can endanger tall RV roofs with solar panels, vents, storage boxes, satellite dishes, and TV antennas.

Another disadvantage in many of these parks is that they are in dense forests and are not conducive to solar panel operation or acquiring satellites for TV viewing. Recently we stopped at a very attractive Forest Service campground in northern California. We wondered why the place was empty until we spoke with the campground host. He said there were several turns in the road that had trees with low branches, and many RVers didn't want to risk their vehicles. He offered to drive Bill around to check one site he thought we might get into. Bill, who has a pretty good eye for evaluating sites, thought we just might be able to make it into the site. With very slow driving, and Jan walking in front of the rig checking constantly side to side, we made it into the site for the night. We were even able to position the trailer so we could use the satellite dish through a hole in the trees.

By and large, it is best to know the situation in any campground before you drive your rig in. If we are interested in a particular unknown campground, we will make a special trip to visit it and check out the conditions, or at least, park outside and take a walking tour of the grounds before we bring in the trailer.

Choosing a Campsite

Once you've determined a campground can accommodate your rig, and you have a choice of campsites, how do you choose the best one? What do you look for? Here are some issues to consider:

- Will the length and width of the site accommodate the size of your RV?
- Is there enough road area to allow you to maneuver your rig into the site?
- Will the angle of the site to the road accommodate your RV?
- Are there any trees in the way to hinder maneuvering?
- If you have a slideout, can you extend it without hitting anything or impinging on an adjacent site?
- Is there anything you could bump into when maneuvering into the site (e.g., posts, poles, trees, shrubs, etc.)?
- Is the site reasonably level—back to front and side to side?
- What is the orientation of the sun? This is especially important if you plan to use solar panels for recharging your batteries. But also keep in mind the heat of the sun. For example, is it shining on the side of the RV where the refrigerator is located? If so, the refrigerator may not cool efficiently or have to work harder.
- Is the tree cover so dense that you won't be able to use the solar panels or the satellite TV? If you use wind power, will the trees block the wind or get in the way of the wind generator?
- Are there low-hanging branches that could scrape or damage your roof or items on the roof? Will branches interfere with the TV antenna when you raise it? Are there any dead branches that might fall during a storm?
- Are there any drainage issues? If you park next to a river or stream, is there a possibility of flooding during a storm? Twice we have almost been marooned by rising water, so we always ask the campground manager about possible flooding, especially flash flooding when there wouldn't time for us to move the RV.
- A well-lit area is good, but will the lights interfere with your sleep?
- Are there buildings nearby that might interfere with breezes?
- What is the view like from your windows and doors?

National Parks

Like the BLM, the National Park Service (NPS) is under the jurisdiction of the Department of the Interior. Created in 1916, the National Park System includes 390 areas comprising more than 84 million acres. Many of our national parks have primitive or dry camping and are good places for boondockers. You can visit the NPS website at www.nps.gov and research the various parks by either park name, state, or activity. Another resource is the *National Park Service Camping Guide*, third edition, by William Herow, which lists nearly 450 campgrounds in 121 national parks.

Army Corps of Engineers Campgrounds

Campgrounds of the Army Corps of Engineers are very nice places to stay. Many grounds have electrical and water hookups, and many do not. The Corps has created over 4,300 recreation areas throughout the country, offering many places for boondock

Enjoying the day at Modoc Campground on J. Strom Thurmond Lake in South Carolina.
(U.S. Army Corps of Engineers/Jonas N. Jordan)

camping. They are usually located on rivers, lakes, reservoirs, or at dam sites, providing fishing and boating activities. Most Corps campgrounds are located in the eastern states where good campgrounds are limited.

Camping with the Corps of Engineers by Spurgeon Hinkle lists campgrounds by state and includes directions, descriptions of facilities, and available activities.

Click on Find a Recreation Area on the home page of the Corps website, www.usace.army.mil, and you'll be directed to a map of the United States. Just click on the state you're interested in, and it will pop up, showing all the campgrounds. Click on a campground, and you'll find a description of the campground and its facilities.

> ## Limited Facilities
>
> Some campgrounds have limited facilities, such as just water or electricity but no other hookups. Although strictly speaking these are not boondock campgrounds, don't discount them as possible campsites. You'll still get to use your boondocking skills. If you have just an electrical hookup, you'll still need to conserve water and keep track of your holding tanks. If you have access to water only, then you'll have to monitor battery consumption and holding tanks.
>
> Also, such campgrounds may be in an urban area as well as a wilderness setting. They may be federal, state, county, or city parks or private camps. Some of our favorite state campsites have had electrical hookups, but no water or sewage at the site. Usually, however, they will have a dump station with a freshwater faucet nearby. We have used this type of campground many, many times.

Local Parks

Many small towns and cities permit dry camping in their parks. We usually try to find these great little parks as we travel. They are not only pretty but usually located in the center of town near stores and shops. We often have camped in the town park in Sheridan, Wyoming, which provides welcome shade on hot summer days with its tall cottonwood trees.

Many counties have excellent parks that only offer dry camping. And while most state parks usually have full hookups, there are a few that only have dry camping, or they may have specific sections of the campground without hookups. In many cases, some of the more popular parks will have a no-hookup overflow section that is used when the rest of the park is full. Camping is often allowed in these areas even if the rest of the park is not completely occupied. In the West, parks for horse trailers (for those doing trail riding) usually allow camping as well.

Highway Overlooks and Rest Areas

Often a pull-off along the highway at a scenic overlook or a historical marker may be a good place to spend the night. We have used such places while traveling, providing they didn't have a sign specifically stating "No overnight parking."

Rest areas along highways are also potential overnight campsites. We find the better rest areas are along the smaller highways and the worse are those on popular interstate highways. The latter have heavier traffic and thus are noisier.

A word of caution: Do not assume a rest area, or campground for that matter, is naturally a safe place. Take some precautions (see the sidebar on page 18).

RVing isn't a dangerous or risky lifestyle. In all our years of RVing, we've never been a victim of any crime, and we've felt secure in most campgrounds. However, a healthy awareness of safety is a good thing.

BOONDOCKING SITES: PRIVATE AND COMMERCIAL PROPERTY

Private Property

Don't discount the possibility of camping on someone's land. We've camped on ranch land as well as along river and stream banks in countless states.

We have camped in many places that were on private land. We never stay on private land unless we've been invited to do so or obtained permission in advance from the owners. Asking strangers to get permission to camp on their property is easy. Just go up to the house and say, "We would like to spend the night in this area. Do you know of any place we could park for the night?" Most people are friendly if you approach them politely. Be neatly dressed, don't look like a person with bad intentions, and you will probably get a good place to stay.

Staying Safe: Security

While we don't want to overemphasize the potential for being a victim of crime, we don't want you to be totally unaware of the possibility. Some suggestions for staying safe are:

- Use common sense when you park your rig. If you boondock in a parking lot or rest area, for example, choose a well-lit, highly visible area.
- Don't use rest-area facilities at night.
- Lock your door when you're inside your RV. If we have the door open for ventilation, we latch the screen door.
- Be suspicious of anyone who knocks on your door at night. Do not immediately open it. Turn on the outside light, use a window to ask for identification (use a flashlight to see it), and find out what they want. If you are uncomfortable with their answers, don't open the door.
- Don't leave valuables unattended around your campsite or in plain sight in your RV or tow vehicle when you leave.
- Lock outside compartments to prevent theft or entry into the RV.
- Close any window near a door to prevent someone from reaching in through the window to open the door.
- Secure motorized vehicles when you leave.

We once wanted to take pictures of Devil's Gate, a natural gorge on the Sweetwater River, on the old Oregon Trail. At the time, it was on the private property of the Sun Ranch (the ranch is now a National Historic Landmark). We went up to the house and inquired if we could walk to the Gate and take some pictures. Mrs. Sun, who was most gracious to us, told us where we could park. We parked, came up to the house later by invitation, enjoyed the cocktail hour, and made some good friends. We stayed four days and had a great time.

Parking Lots

As mentioned in Chapter 1, most RVers practice convenience camping, staying in a parking lot overnight and moving on the next day. A long drive, weariness, or full campgrounds are some of the reasons to pull into a parking lot. And there are a lot of options with this type of boondocking, as we'll cover below.

Retail Stores and Restaurants

Retail and chain stores often have large, well-lit parking lots. We have camped at Fred Meyer, Kmart, and Wal-Mart stores (or Camp Wally as they are more commonly called). In fact, Wal-Mart carries an edition of the Rand McNally road atlas with an insert that lists all the U.S. and Canadian Wal-Marts. Other options might include discount warehouses, such as Sam's Club, or restaurants, such as Cracker Barrel and McDonald's.

The first step of course is to talk with the store manager or owner to get permission to boondock and find out where you can park. Wearing neat, clean clothes goes a long way to making a good first impression and reassuring the manager/owner. Sometimes such courtesy can lead to perks. He or she may suggest you plug an electrical cord into a convenient outlet. When we've availed ourselves of this offer, we make sure to not run our air conditioner unless we know that no other equipment is running on the same circuit. In northern climes, retail places often have electrical outlets so customers can plug in the engine-block heaters on their vehicles during cold weather, and a kind owner might suggest you use one of them.

Other courtesies include parking in the spot they've selected, keeping your campsite clean, and staying only as long as they've allowed. It is always a good idea and good manners to patronize the store or restaurant while you're parked in their lot—it goes a long way toward saying thank-you.

Once when we were traveling near a small town, we hit a bad bump and broke a spring on the trailer. We limped into the town and found a convenient motel with a large parking lot. We parked the rig in a back corner, and I went in to see the manager. I explained my problem to him and asked if we could stay there until we could find someone to fix it. He said yes, we could stay, and offered names of people we could contact for help. We drove around, but the best we could do was order another spring from the manufacturer, which would take four days to arrive. I was worried about staying that long, but the motel manager said we could stay, and even offered his son as a helper. Between the two of us we fixed the axle quickly once the spring arrived, and the RV was ready to get back on the road. I gave $10 to the son, and offered some money to the manager, but he said we owed him nothing. What nice people!

Casinos

Casinos are excellent places for convenience camping. We don't know of any casinos that prohibit overnight camping, unless they have a commercial campground. Of course, they expect you to patronize the facilities, so at least eat in their restaurants, which often have excellent buffets at reasonable prices. We stop and sample the food and the slots occasionally. If you do use the parking lot for camping, try to park at the outer fringes of the lot so you won't be in the way of their higher-spending patrons. Do not abuse the privilege by staying more than a few days unless management has approved it, or by dumping trash or, do we dare mention it, gray water on the ground or pavement. With the profusion of casinos being built all over the country, they can make great overnight stops with good food and entertainment. Some casinos have regular RV parks, but still allow boondocking in certain areas of the parking lot.

Code of Conduct

It is an unfortunate truth that some RVers can make a mess of a parking lot. This became apparent to us during a recent trip to Alaska.

There are only a few private campgrounds in the city of Anchorage, and most of them are small and usually full. Consequently, it is a necessity for people to boondock in retail store parking lots, such as Wal-Mart, Kmart, and Fred Meyer stores. Kmart left a slip of paper under our windshield wiper, stating that we were welcome to stay for three days.

Unfortunately, we saw many RVers who had left trashbags lying on the ground. We wondered whether this would cause problems in the future, and we have heard from friends that Alaskan Wal-Marts have banned overnight RV parking because RVers have spoiled the privilege.

For these business establishments to allow us the privilege of staying in their parking lots, we RVers must exhibit good manners and follow certain rules. The Escapees RV Club promotes a Code of Conduct (RVers' Good Neighbor Policy) to help make our stays more palatable. It is endorsed by The Escapees RV Club, Family Motor Coach Association, Wally Bynam Caravan Club, Gulf Streamers, and Life on Wheels (LoW).

1. Stay one night only!
2. Obtain permission from a qualified individual.
3. Obey posted regulations.
4. No awnings, chairs, or barbecue grills.
5. Do not use hydraulic jacks on soft surfaces (including asphalt).
6. Always leave an area cleaner than you found it.
7. Purchase gas, food, or supplies as a form of thank-you, when feasible.
8. Be safe! Always be aware of your surroundings, and leave if you feel unsafe.

Additionally, it's courteous to arrive after rush-hour traffic, park out of the way (e.g., on the edges of the lot) while also leaving a buffer between your RV and nearby homes, and leave your slideouts in until nightfall.

Small courtesies will make your stay more enjoyable, for both you and your host.

Truck Stops

We have often stopped at truck stops, such as Flying J. They offer hookups, restaurants, and showers.

We've also camped in parking lots at Elks and Moose lodges, since we are members.

Friends and Relatives

Finally, most RVers like to stay with relatives sometimes, parking in their driveways. This can require that you dry camp if they cannot provide water and electric service. Usually you can run an extension cord from the house or garage to your RV. However, your hosts will probably not have the ability to provide a sewer drain, so you'll need to conserve water to avoid having to empty your holding tanks during your visit.

HOW TO FIND BOONDOCKING SITES

There are many places to boondock, and we have tried to list some of the most popular ones. But how do you start to compile information on your own list of sites?

Maps and Directories

We are great map collectors and have many detailed maps of certain areas, particularly the national forest areas of the West. Our favorite maps and directories are those from USFS, BLM, and NPS offices and ranger stations. They show the locations of back-road campgrounds and include many campgrounds not shown on regular AAA and auto travel maps or in major camping directories.

We look at our maps often, and if we find a likely looking campground, we'll make a special trip to the location without our trailer or inquire at a ranger station or other government office to find out if we can get into the camp. When we find a good place, we mark it on the map so we'll remember it and also list it in our logbook. In this way, we've compiled our own list of suitable campgrounds.

Another way to find good boondock campgrounds is to pick up official state maps (see below for how to get these). We also get a copy of the state's campground directory. These two publications together will usually list all the recreation areas as well as the state, county, and city parks where camping is available.

The Internet

The Internet is a cornucopia of information on campgrounds, parks, types of camping available, as well as fees, reservation and contact information, frequently asked questions (FAQs), and just about anything else you might need. Many state sites have online maps for their parks and recreation areas; at the very least, they will have contact information so you can call to obtain a printed map. Search for "state of" for the state you want to visit, then go that state's home page. Usually you will find a button for Visitors, Recreation, Travel, Tourism, or something similar, which will take you to what is available. Parks and campgrounds will be listed there.

If you have a particular campground, park, or forest in mind, it may have its own website, where you can find the specific information you need. Keep in mind, however, that most primitive sites will not be listed.

Other Boondockers

Boondockers share a great sense of camaraderie, and most are all too happy to share their knowledge of good and bad campgrounds. (Many boondockers and RVers even have their own websites and may enjoy corresponding via e-mail. Search for "boondockers" or a variation.)

Over the years, we've developed quite a list of our own favorite campgrounds, scattered throughout the country. These sites range from ocean beaches to 9,000-foot-high mountain valleys. Often they are many miles from civilization, which gives us a wonderful feeling of adventure. To start you off on your own list, following are some of our favorite campsites:

- Lamoille Canyon is about 20 miles south of Elko, Nevada, on a well-marked road. The Thomas Canyon Campground is located at the 7,000-foot level in the canyon and has a paved road up to the 9,000-foot level, where there are restroom facilities, water, and several hiking trails into the Ruby Mountains. There are several sites near the campground entrance big enough for large rigs. The loop road also has sites available, but it is best to inspect them before pulling into the road. If you climb the rocks in back of the camp to the hanging canyon above, you'll find a pretty trail. It is a great place to visit in the fall.

- Hoback River area, located along Highway 191/26, south of Jackson Hole, Wyoming. You'll find several good campsites on this stretch of road.

- North along Highway 352 west and north of Pinedale, Wyoming.

- Bighorn Mountains campsites are located along Highways 14 or 16, either north or south of Sheridan, Wyoming—*if* you can make the climb up into the mountains with your rig (be sure to check first). ***Do not*** enter or leave the mountains from the west side because of extremely steep roads (grades of 10% to 15%).

- Big Hole River, on Highway 43 between the towns of Divide and Wisdom in Montana. Fishermen

The hanging canyon at Lamoille Canyon, Nevada, which you can reach by following the trail from the campground.

especially will enjoy the many campgrounds along this river.

- Bitterroot Valley, along U.S. Highway 93 in Montana. There are lots of campgrounds and recreation areas in this valley. Additionally, the Bitterroot National Forest, with its own campgrounds, surrounds the valley.

- Willamette National Forest and Three Sisters Wilderness along Highways 22 and 126 east of Salem or Eugene, Oregon. This forest is part of the Cascades Range in Oregon, and you'll find campgrounds in the forest and along these highways.

- Oregon coast has many great campgrounds, including two of our favorites: Cape Lookout State Park, west of Portland, Oregon, off U.S. Highway 101; and South Beach State Park, south of Newport on U.S. Highway 101.

Although we have been to all these campgrounds, please keep in mind that places change, and these may have changed since we last visited. If you search the Internet for any of these areas or campgrounds, you'll find more detailed and up-to-date information. We've also included an appendix at the end of the book with a state-by-state listing of some of our favorite boondocking campgrounds.

American Automobile Association

We highly recommend membership in the American Automobile Association (AAA). Their campground directories list many boondock government campgrounds you will not find in other directories. They have superior maps that are free to members. In addition, AAA tour books list good restaurants and almost all the places of interest in an area.

Finally we would not travel anywhere without a AAA TripTik, easy-to-read strip maps of approximately 200-mile sections of your trip (interstates and major highways), which give you all the traveling information you need to sort out the interstate highway system. It's easy to calculate mileage from either end of the strip, using the scale on the strip. They show exit numbers as well as the services found at each exit (identified by symbols). All the strips are contained in a spiral binder in the order of your trip. Once you are a member, just contact the AAA with your travel plans, and they'll compile a TripTik specifically for your trip.

Escapees Magazine

The Escapees RV Club publishes *Escapees*, a monthly magazine that is a good resource for any RVer, and for boondockers in particular. "Day's End" is a monthly column written by Bob and Viva Lee Ed that lists boondocking sites sent in by club members. Many of these locations are very good ones. However, when visiting these sites, or planning to, keep in mind that neither the Club nor the columnists have inspected these sites, and what is a good site for one RVer may not be a good site for you. The Eds have compiled a directory of these sites, which is available to Escapees members; go to www.escapees.com/daysend/index.asp for more information.

Local Police Stations

Years ago when we were in Maine, we met a charming elderly woman traveling alone in a 29-foot travel trailer pulled by an ancient car. When she arrived in a town, her practice was to go to the police station, explain that she was traveling alone, and ask where she could park for the night. Usually she would be told to park in a given grocery store or shopping center parking lot, and the police would call the manager or owner to tell them she would be there. They would also send a patrol car around periodically during the night to see if she was all right. This was almost twenty years ago, and you may not always get the same courtesy and solicitousness today, but police stations are still good places to ask for suggestions.

We do know of a town in upstate New York where you can register at the police station with the desk sergeant for an overnight parking spot. And if you visit the police station in Arcadia, California, the desk sergeant will assign you a spot with an electrical hookup for a modest fee.

We'll end this chapter with one more story of a place we once stayed. We were traveling in Nebraska, doing research for the book we were currently working on, and couldn't find any place to camp. While we were driving through one small town, we spotted an auto parts store with a good-sized parking lot. Bill asked the manager if we could camp in the back of the lot. He said yes, we could, but preferred that we park in front. You see, it was Saturday night, and he thought we might keep the local drunks from breaking his windows. And he was right—there were no broken windows during the two days we were there.

CHAPTER 3

Selecting a Rig

When we decided to fulltime in 1982, we wanted to be able to continue the boondock camping experiences we had previously enjoyed. While we were still in the planning stages and studying what type of RV to buy, we gathered as many maps and campground directories as we could find to learn the locations of all the best primitive campgrounds. We noticed that many of the most interesting campgrounds had restrictions regarding RV size. Based on our findings, we decided that an RV no longer than 25 feet would probably be best for our needs since our primary goal was boondock camping. We settled for a 23-foot travel trailer, which served us well for eight years of fulltime living and allowed us to do a lot of boondock camping along the way.

Eventually we needed far more space for our writing and photographic equipment, so we decided a larger trailer was in order. We found a 29-foot, fifth-wheel trailer that suited our storage and living needs, although we regretted that we could no longer visit many of our favorite small campgrounds.

(RVIA)

WHAT'S AVAILABLE?

Obviously, the main piece of equipment you need for easy boondocking is a suitable RV. However, before you can choose an RV that suits you, it helps to know what's available. So let's review the types of RVs.

Recreational vehicles include the following:

- Folding tent trailers (or pop-up trailers)

- Camping van conversions (Class B motorhomes)

- Pickup campers

- Travel trailers (conventional and fifth-wheel)

- Class A motorhomes

- Class C motorhomes (mini-motorhomes)

Our first fulltiming RV at Valley of Fire State Park in Nevada while we were boondocking.

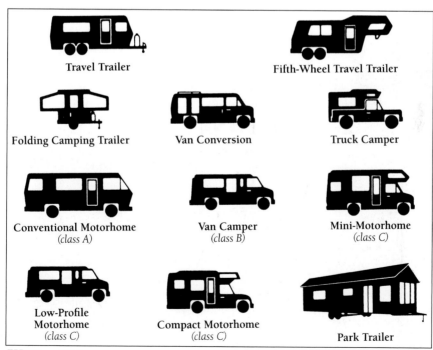

Travel Trailer

Fifth-Wheel Travel Trailer

Folding Camping Trailer

Van Conversion

Truck Camper

Conventional Motorhome
(class A)

Van Camper
(class B)

Mini-Motorhome
(class C)

Low-Profile Motorhome
(class C)

Compact Motorhome
(class C)

Park Trailer

RV types. (RVIA)

For our boondocking purposes, we'll focus on pickup campers, travel trailers, and motorhomes. The small size of tent trailers and camping vans, as well as the fact that they are not self-contained (see Chapter 4), do not make them good candidates for boondocking.

Pickup Campers

A pickup camper, the smallest boondocking RV, is installed in the bed of a pickup truck. Manufacturers are designing these campers for true boondocking, making allowances and space for solar panels, several batteries, chargers, bathrooms with showers, and other goodies. The newer ones offer all the conveniences of bigger rigs, including slideouts, which do improve the space in these units.

Advantages of pickup campers are:

- They can go where no other RV can go—right up the mountainside on a four-wheel-drive trail.

- You can remove the camper from the truck with hydraulic jacks and set it up at the campsite.

- With the camper detached, you can use the truck as transportation so you don't need to tow a separate vehicle.

Disadvantages of pickup campers are:

- They are cramped, and many people find them too claustrophobic for long-term use.

- They lack storage, severely limiting what you can take with you.

The interior of a Host pickup camper, a layout suited for boondocking.

With a pickup camper, your "home" is installed in the bed of the truck. (RVIA)

■ Removing the camper from the truck to set up at a campsite is a chore. You must disconnect many things, including all the electrical connections. Pickup-camper RVers tell us it is not something you would want to do all the time.

However, if the lack of space is not a problem for you, this RV might be worth considering.

Travel Trailers

Towable trailers include the conventional trailer and the fifth-wheel trailer.

A conventional travel trailer. (RVIA)

The tow vehicle of a conventional trailer must be equipped with a weight-distributing hitch, an antisway control, and safety chains. The heaviest of the hitches can handle up to 14,000 pounds of trailer weight.

Advantages of conventional trailers are:

■ They can sleep up to eight people, depending on model and floorplan.

■ Their affordability and ease of use make them a good choice for a first RV.

Disadvantages of conventional trailers are:

■ They are hard to back into a campsite.

■ The hitching process is quite complicated.

■ The interior space can be quite compact, and most often the beds are convertible models.

■ You have to be careful of the swaying issue, and they can be hard to maneuver in traffic.

Fifth-wheel trailers are the choice of most fulltimers, and are probably the most popular RVs for boondocking. It has an elevated front, called a gooseneck, which projects over the bed of the pickup-truck tow vehicle, adding living space. Under the gooseneck is the kingpin, which is considered the "fifth wheel"; it fits into a hitch in the bed of the pickup truck. These hitches are quite heavy and can weigh 700 pounds or more. They are available in various sizes up to a capacity of 24,000 pounds.

Advantages of fifth-wheel trailers are:

- They are easy to back into a campsite.

- They have a good amount of interior room.

- They do not have a swaying problem on the road, and are quite maneuverable in traffic.

Disadvantages of fifth-wheel trailers are:

- The wheels of the trailer cut a tighter circle than the truck wheels when turning, which can cause the trailer wheels to jump over curbs if you cut the corners too closely.

These versatile trailers come in many sizes, and they have a surprising amount of storage space. We took a 21-foot (no slide) Nash to Alaska, and it was very comfortable for the two of us during our four-month journey.

However, Jan didn't think that she could live in a 21-foot trailer fulltime, so we now have a 34-footer with two slideouts. We are finding more and more people living in huge RVs, such as one couple we know who live in a 42-footer towed by a heavy-duty Peterbilt truck with a sleeper cab. Most of the newer, larger fifth-wheel units cannot be pulled by a standard 1-ton pickup truck anymore because of the extra weight. These large trailers are as large as a house, with all the bells and whistles. They have generators and solar panels to provide power for all their electrical needs and huge battery banks to store it. And the amazing thing is that many of these people boondock all the time.

Motorhomes

One of the best RVs for boondocking is a small, well-equipped Class A or Class C motorhome with a built-in generator. Some of the largest motorhomes are bus conversions; i.e., the chassis, frame, and engine of a bus form the basic structure. Class C models are built on a van chassis and have a cabover bunk.

Our 21-foot Nash fifth-wheel trailer at a park in Canada.

A fifth-wheel family enjoying the good life. (RVIA)

Advantages of motorhomes are:

■ They usually have good-sized water and waste tanks.

■ They come with built-in generators, which allow you to use TVs, a microwave, computers, and heaters. A generator will also charge batteries and run an air conditioner (a luxury many RVers want occasionally). The built-in generator is where motorhomes shine over trailers.

Disadvantages of motorhomes are:

■ Most motorhome owners tow a car for local transportation and making short trips from the campsite. This means you have to maintain, license, and insure a second vehicle.

■ If you don't want to tow a car, then you need to break camp each time you must go somewhere.

■ They are expensive compared to travel trailers.

A Class A motorhome is a great way to see the country. (RVIA)

A Class A motorhome is a good choice for family boondocking trips. (RVIA)

A Class C motorhome also makes a good boondocking RV. (RVIA)

A Class C motorhome can take you right where you want to go. (RVIA)

A good friend of ours, Sharlene Minshall, has driven a small 27-foot Class A motorhome for seventeen years. She bought it new, and it has served her well, including three solo trips to Alaska and a lot of boondocking. Just recently, she bought another small motorhome to replace the older one.

SELECTING YOUR RIG

Now that you know the types of rigs available, let's look at some other factors to consider in selecting a rig.

Personal Factors

Your rig has to fit your needs, wants, and your resources, all of which are personal and unique to you and your family. We can't identify these for anyone; however, here are some questions to help you get started:

- What is your budget?
- Do you want to go used or new?
- What fuel do you prefer, diesel or gas?
- How many people will be regularly camping in the RV?
- Will you be RVing part-time or fulltime?
- If part-time, how much time will you spend RVing, and of that time, how much will be boondocking?
- Will you take your pets?
- Where will you park your RV when not on the road? Are there any town or city ordinances that you need to be aware of?

A good way to begin your research for a new RV is to visit RV shows and dealerships. Walk through the models, try out the chairs and beds, sit on the toilet with the door closed, stand in the shower, and check the height of the kitchen counters and sink. Really poke around and get a feel for how the RV fits you. Do you have children? Bring them along and let them wander about while you stand in the kitchen. Is the rig too small? Does the layout work for your whole family? Is there enough seating for the whole family to sit down at one time?

While you're there, also pick up brochures and product literature. If there's room, make notes on the literature about what you like, questions you have about a specific model, and what does and doesn't work. Or bring a notepad for this information. After going through a few RVs, the details will probably start to blend together, and your notes will come in handy.

Then we suggest you go home and study the information you've collected to begin narrowing down the specifications and features you need and want in your RV. When you've got a good idea of what you are looking for, then revisit the show or dealership to get more specific information for the particular RV(s) you're considering, as well as information on customization and financing.

Size and Design

While you may think you want as large an RV as you can afford, if you want to boondock, remember to pay attention to the length and width of the RV. As we related at the beginning of this chapter, before purchasing a new RV, we researched the campgrounds we wanted to visit and the RV dimensions they would accommodate. If you choose an RV that is too long or too wide, it will not be able to negotiate the roads in many public campgrounds, especially those in many national forests.

Additionally, RVs with slideouts may not fit into many of the sites in these campgrounds with the slideout extended. We know that today it is heresy to criticize big RVs with large slideouts, but they do prevent your using a great many campsites. Today it is almost impossible to buy a new RV without a slideout, and most rigs now have multiple slides; two are standard, and three, four, and even five are becoming more common. The main disadvantages of slideouts are their extra weight, which impacts fuel consumption, and the space they require to extend. You must make allowances when parking so slideouts won't hit a tree or other campground equipment when they are extended.

In the end, selecting an RV for boondock camping is purely a personal decision. It really doesn't matter if you have a Class A motorhome or a pickup camper as long as it's what you want and are comfortable with. I don't consider a tent camper a proper boondocking RV because they lack large water and holding tanks, but I have friends who have boondocked in one for many years. My nephew just recently purchased a combi-type hard-sided trailer with cloth slideout beds at each end. He and his wife plan to do a lot of primitive camping. Choose whatever you can afford, and whatever makes you happy.

CHAPTER 4

Water, Sewage, and Trash

Successful boondocking requires that we manage resources—water, propane, and power—as well as waste. In this chapter, we'll cover managing our water supply, sewage, and trash. We'll cover propane in Chapter 5, and power in the electrical chapters.

WATER

Water is probably the most important item in boondock camping. Without it you can't wash, shave, cook, or clean. Plus you also need water to drink. The question is how much water will you need?

(RVIA)

At home, we use a great deal of water, probably without even thinking about it. The New York City Department of Environmental Protection reports on its website (www.nyc.gov/html/dep/html/residents/wateruse.shtml) that the national average indoor residential water use per day per person is 60 to 70 gallons of water. Depending upon your rig,

Table 4-1. How Long Will the Water Supply Last?			
Water Supply (gallons)	1 person	2 people	4 people
40	6 days	3 days	1 1/2 days
60	10 days	5 days	2 1/2 days
80	13 days	6 1/2 days	3 days
100	16 days	8 days	4 days

your freshwater tank could range in size from 40 to 90 gallons. And if there are two people using that water supply, you can easily see how we boondockers must look at water use in a different way. Conservation, at least when boondocking, has to be a way of life.

So how much water do we use when boondocking? For the two of us, when we are actively conserving (including a few skimpy showers), we use about 6 gallons per day per person. Our 60-gallon water tank can last us five days or more. Based upon this, we've put together Table 4-1 to give you a quick estimate of how long a freshwater supply might last for different numbers of RVers. And we say "might" because matters of use and conservation will vary greatly from person to person.

Conserving Water

Throughout our years of fulltiming and boondocking, we've experimented with different ways of reducing our water usage. Here are a few ideas:

■ Never turn on a faucet and just let the water run. If you're waiting for the water to get hot, capture the cold water to use elsewhere.

■ When washing your hands, wet them, shut off the water, soap up, and then rinse.

■ Instead of using water to wash hands, use a waterless hand sanitizing product or baby wipes for messier jobs. The latter is a trade-off because you'll be adding to the trash, but with children, the trade-off may be worth it.

■ Install a showerhead shutoff valve if you have a showerhead that cannot be completely turned off. We installed a Water Whiz ball valve with female 1/2-inch pipe threads on each end, although any shutoff valve will work with the proper fittings. We got ours at Home Depot. This valve is made of white PVC and has a large, easy-to-grip handle for turning the spray on and off. It also matches the color of most white hoses and showerheads. To install:
  1. You will also need a close nipple with a 1/2-inch pipe thread to assemble the unit.
  2. Put some pipe dope on the threads of the close nipple and screw it in one end of the valve.
  3. Attach the unit between the showerhead and the hose.

Having a good way to turn off the water flow at the showerhead allows you to get wet, turn off the water, lather up, turn on the water, and rinse without altering the hot/cold water setting. We measured the amount of water once, and we can each shower in 1 gallon of water. It's hard to do, but it can be done.

■ To get the shower water to the right temperature without a lot of adjusting, mark each knob in increments with varying lengths of colored tape. This will give you a guide as to where the knob should be set.

■ Take sponge baths. During a recent hospital stay for surgery, Bill discovered a great product called No-Rinse Body Bath (www.norinse.com). It was developed for NASA astronauts. Squirt 1 ounce into a small container of water and wash with a washcloth. It doesn't lather, so you don't have to rinse it off, although you can rinse if you want. It leaves the skin clean and odor free. Jan has even washed her hair with it and liked the smell of it. You can also purchase No-Rinse Shampoo and No-Rinse Wipes. The website lists retailers who carry these products; even more convenient and perhaps cheaper, go to your Wal-Mart pharmacy, and if they don't stock it, they will special-order them for you. Check your local pharmacies as well.

■ Install single-lever faucets in the bathroom and galley sinks. These can adjust the faucet to the proper temperature without wasting a lot of water.

■ Before washing the dishes, wipe them as clean as you can with paper towels.

■ Don't fill the sink with water to wash the dishes. Use the largest pan or bowl that you have previously used in preparing the meal as a dishpan. Use another container for the rinse water and dip the dishes in it instead of pouring water over them.

■ Use paper plates and bowls, and dispose of them by burning them in a fire pit, if the campsite has one.

■ Prepare foods that use as little water as possible for cooking and avoid those that use a lot, such as pasta. (You can cook pasta and similar foods before you go boondocking.)

■ Steam or microwave foods when you can, especially vegetables.

Replenishing Your Water Supply

If your freshwater capacity isn't large enough to last through a period of boondocking even with conservation, you have several options for replenishing your freshwater supply.

Carry Extra Water with You

The first option is to carry extra water in jugs. We carry two 6-gallon jerry jugs with water just for this purpose. If you intend to transfer the water in the jugs into the tank on your RV, keep in mind that large-sized jugs are heavy and may be difficult to handle when full. Also, using a funnel will usually make the job go quicker—and with less spillage—than pouring directly from a jug.

Campground Water Source

Some boondock campgrounds have communal faucets providing potable water. If your campsite is close enough, you might be able to reach the faucet with your hose. Otherwise, you'll have to take either your RV or jugs to the faucet. (To be courteous, don't leave your hose connected to such a faucet for any longer than it takes to fill your tank.)

Often these faucets will not have threads on the end of the spout so that a hose cannot be connected in the normal manner (this is done deliberately to discourage greedy water users from hooking up to the faucet). A water thief will help for these situations. This device has a rubber sleeve on one end to slip over the smooth faucet spout and a hose fitting at the other end to attach your hose to.

Portable Water Tanks

If you wish to dry camp for long periods of time in a certain area, you can use a portable bladder water tank to transport water from a nearby town or water source to your RV. These tanks are made of flexible PVC and are available in sizes from 13 to 35 gallons. Bladder tanks were designed for use in boats during long ocean passages, and they are ideal for boondocking.

You can transfer the water from the bladder tank to your RV tank with a 12-volt water pump (the kind used for pressurizing your RV's water system). Connect it to the 1/2-inch outlet fitting on the bladder tank. Or you can use a gravity feed or siphon.

While at Quartzsite one year, we saw a flexible tank lashed on the roof of a pickup truck's cab, which probably gave the tank a high enough position for a gravity feed to work. You could also mount such a tank in the bed of a pickup truck or on the roof of a car or a sport utility vehicle, using a 12-volt water pump to transfer the water into your main tank.

You can purchase bladder tanks from RV supply stores or boating supply houses such as West Marine. The extra 12-volt DC water pump used with the tank can also serve as a spare in case the main pump in the RV's water system breaks down.

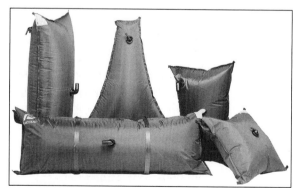
You can use flexible water tanks to transport water to the RV. (Navimo and West Marine)

Hard-sided polyethylene water tanks are also an option that you could mount in a truck bed or a car's trunk for the same purpose.

HOLDING TANKS

As we mentioned earlier, your RV must be self-contained for boondocking, meaning you must have not only a freshwater tank,

Table 4-2. Standard Holding Tank Sizes		
RV Type	Gray-Water Tank (gallons)	Black-Water Tank (gallons)
Fifth-wheel trailer	30–80	40–80
Class A motorhome	43–75	40–75
Class C motorhome	30–50	30–50

but also holding tanks for the liquid and solid wastes. The ideal setup is to have a gray-water tank for the liquids coming from the sink and shower and a black-water tank for the toilet waste. The gray-water tank should be the larger of the two, as it will fill faster. It is never a good idea to have only one holding tank as it will fill up quickly and need to be emptied more often.

Table 4-2 provides some standard holding tank sizes for fifth-wheel trailers and motorhomes. Specific sizes will vary from model to model and among manufacturers, so use these only as general guidelines.

By reducing your water consumption, you not only extend your freshwater supply, you also minimize the amount of water that goes into your gray-water holding tank. You can further reduce filling up the gray-water tank by using some gray water to flush the toilet.

There are several steps you can take to reduce the quantity of waste that goes into your black-water holding tank as well. For example:

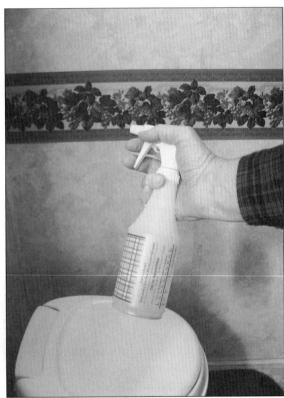

- Use a spray bottle filled with water to remove any remaining traces of waste left in the bowl rather than flushing more than once. (The permanent sprayer mounted on the side of some RV toilets uses too much water to be practical for long-term boondocking.) We first tried the spray bottles found in cosmetic departments but the spraying mechanism broke down too quickly. Now we buy spray bottles from garden departments, which are sturdier and have a more forceful spray.

Conserve water by using a common spray bottle, available from any garden shop, to clean the toilet bowl.

■ Keep a small bag in the bathroom to collect toilet paper so that none of it goes into the holding tank, then burn the bag in the fire pit. There's no danger of spreading germs if it's burned completely. If you can't burn it, close the bag securely and dispose of it in a trash receptacle. If this offends your sensibilities, consider that the toilet paper holds less waste than a loaded disposable diaper, which are commonly disposed of in this manner.

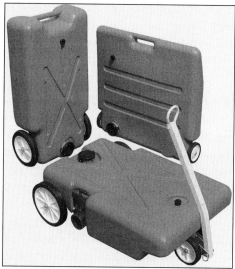

Portable holding tanks allow you to transport waste to a dump station.
(Barker Manufacturing)

Portable Holding Tanks

For long-term boondocking, it may be more practical to have a means of taking your waste to a nearby dump station rather than breaking camp to take the RV. Many small towns located near popular boondocking areas have public dump stations. Service stations also may have dump stations available for a small fee.

Portable holding tanks can be mounted in the same manner as water tanks on trucks or other vehicles. Then you can use your macerator pump (see below) to both fill the portable tank at the RV and empty it at a dump station. Holding tanks are available in sizes from 5 to 32 gallons. Two companies that make these are Barker Manufacturing (Tote-Alongs; www.barkermfg.com) and Coast Distribution System (Tote-N-Stor; www.coastdistribution.com). The larger ones, which are very heavy when full, have optional equipment that allows you to hitch one to your tow vehicle or dinghy so you can tow it to the dump.

The problem with a tote is that it may not hold as much as one of your holding tanks. And once the gate valve is open, you may not be able to get it closed fast enough to keep the tote from overflowing. To avoid this problem, it is best to empty the holding tanks often, before they get too full.

Do not dump holding tanks, even gray water, on the ground or down a gopher hole, or by digging a large hole to hold the

Staying Safe: Sewage Overflow

Keep in mind that if your black-water tank overflows, you are dealing with human waste, which carries microorganisms that can make you sick if ingested. Be careful to use a disinfectant to thoroughly clean your hands and anything else that gets contaminated by waste from the black-water tank.

waste. Years ago this was acceptable, but today there is too much pollution in the groundwater as it is, and your waste water can contaminate someone's drinking well or even your own source of drinking water. We believe it is the duty of all boondockers to help protect the water supply.

Macerator Pumps

You can also avoid overfilling the tote by using a macerator pump. This device is mounted on a flat sewage cap (replacing the existing cap) that fits on the end of the sewer pipe and runs on 12-volt power. The pump grinds the waste in your holding tank (including the toilet paper) as it pumps the waste through the hose. You can control the flow into the tote simply by switching the macerator pump on and off.

Macerators also allow fast discharge of your holding tanks at dump stations as they can suck a reasonably large tank dry in just a few minutes. You can also replace the flimsy sewer hoses with a good-quality $3/4$-inch garden hose or a 1-inch washing machine hose.

Macerator pumps can be very handy. For example, if your campsite is close enough to a dump station, you may be able to use the macerator pump and a very long hose to empty your holding tanks without breaking camp. Or if you're visiting friends or relatives in your RV you may be able to use the pump to dump your holding tanks into the cleanout fitting of the house sewer pipe, although it is a hassle. These fittings are often located outdoors or in the basement of the house.

We have only one word of caution: Macerator pumps are impeller pumps, and they can burn out if allowed to run dry. Be sure to shut off the pump once the tank is empty.

TRASH

Managing trash is an important issue for boondockers. As consumers, we can generate quite a bit of it, and it can become a problem for boondockers. First, we have less space for trash containers, and second, disposal can be more challenging—there are no trash pickups for us!

Reduce the Trash You Take with You

If you are a part-time RVer, prevention is a good place to start with trash management—eliminate as much potential trash as you can before you leave home. See what foodstuffs you can put into reusable containers (with a secure lid) or plastic bags. For example, dry cereals, canned foods, and baking items (such as cake or muffin mixes) can go into

> ### Staying Safe: Keep Your Campsite Clean
>
> If you're boondocking in a wilderness area, such as a national forest, it is important to keep your campsite clean of trash and garbage. You're not only closer to nature in these places, but closer to wildlife, and the smell of trash or garbage can bring uninvited animal visitors into your campsite.

plastic containers or bags. If you're taking boxed frozen vegetables, dispose of the box at home (in your recycle bin!) and just take the plastic bag of vegetables.

Getting Rid of Trash

When you get to your campsite, the easiest way to get rid of trash is to put it in the campground's own trash containers—if it provides them. Or you may be able to burn most of your trash in a fire pit.

If these options aren't available, you'll have to keep it with you until you leave. This requires that you have a trash storage area. Since recycling is common and even required in many areas, you will need to plan this trash area to allow for some separation of trash. For example, have a separate container for cans, bottles, and paper/garbage. Compress what trash you can as much as possible to keep it from overwhelming you.

CHAPTER 5

Food: Stocking, Cooking, and Storing

As far as boondock camping is concerned, cooking and storing food are pretty much the same as any other type of RVing. However, you'll want to look at menu planning with an eye toward conserving your resources, such as water, propane, or battery power, especially if you're doing extended boondocking. This will be reflected in what foods you stock and how you cook them.

PROPANE SUPPLY

First let's start with a primer on propane, which you'll use for the stove/oven, refrigerator, and hot-water heater. (Heaters also use propane—see Chapter 6.) Propane, also called liquefied

(RVIA)

petroleum gas, or LPG, is a flammable, colorless, odorless gas. It is compressed to a liquid, then stored and transported in cylinders.

The propane we buy in cylinders for our RVs isn't 100% propane; it can contain other chemicals such as propylene, butane, and ethylene. Because it is an odorless gas, ethanethiol (also known as ethyl mercaptan) also is added to give it the characteristic rotten egg smell.

Because propane is flammable, propane fires and explosions are always a risk. When handled properly, however, propane is a safe fuel for heating, cooking, and cooling.

With its gas lines, valves, and tanks, an RV's propane system has a lot of potential for leaks to occur. When you combine this with the vibration and stress of road travel, it is wise to regularly check for leaks.

To do this, fill a spray bottle with soapy water and spray on line and valve connections and along gas lines. If you see bubbles, there is a leak. (You can also purchase liquid products from RV supply stores that perform this same function.) Make repairs immediately. **Do not use your propane system until you've fixed all leaks!** There are also some propane detectors available; Camping World (www.campingworld.com) offers a selection.

It's also a good idea to have your propane system inspected annually by a qualified propane gas or RV dealer.

STOCKING THE PANTRY

When stocking your RV, a variety of types of food is a good idea. You'll want some foods that have a long shelf life and need no refrigeration, for example:

- Dry cereal and crackers
- Peanut butter and jelly (unopened)
- Canned goods: meats, tuna, vegetables, fruits, juices, soups, and desserts
- Dry milk (package in self-sealing or zip-top plastic bags to make pints or quarts of milk)
- Instant coffee and tea bags
- Sugar and powdered coffee creamer
- Snacks, such as canned or packaged nuts, raisins and dried fruit, granola, and breakfast bars

Supplement canned and packaged foods with fresh produce, bread, meat, and baked goods. Stopping at a grocery store before you pull into a campground can provide you with fresh food for a couple of days. Also, check out farm stands and orchards where you can pick the fruit yourself. It's a great way to get to know the people in the area and have fun as well.

And sometimes, you can find unexpected bounty. Once when we were in a very remote place, we found a hill loaded with ripe blueberries. We picked and picked until we had nearly filled a large bucket with berries. When we got back to the RV, we were not quite sure what to do with them until we decided to bake a couple of pies. We finally baked a total of three and a half (one small) pies, and gorged ourselves on them for breakfast, lunch, dinner, and late-night snacks. We finally had to leave the place when we ran out of flour. Events like this make for great boondocking memories.

If you are not a fulltimer, you'll have the opportunity before your RV trip to do some preparation. Make the most of your storage space and propane supply by planning your meals ahead of time. Precook whatever you can and package securely (remember, however, that space in an RV refrigerator is much less than in a typical home fridge). Planning meals ahead may seem to take the spontaneity out of boondocking, but it prevents you from forgetting something or taking more than you need and wasting valuable storage space. By planning, you can also manage your water and propane, so you don't run out of cooking fuel when there are still three days to go in your camping schedule. However, it's always a good idea to have ingredients for supplies you don't need to cook in case you do run out of cooking fuel and would rather not break camp.

COOKING

Cooking meals can be as fancy or as simple as you'd like when you're boondocking. And you may find some really creative ways to produce family meals. Obviously, using the stove and oven in your RV is one way to prepare meals; the microwave is another. Sometimes cooking food for a few minutes in the microwave, such as frozen vegetables, is a more efficient use of resources than boiling them on the stove. And don't forget your charcoal grill where you can enjoy cooking outdoors.

But you might want to use this time creatively as well by supplementing the usual cooking methods with the unusual. For example, try campfire cooking. The pioneers did it using good old-fashioned cast-iron cookware. If your campsite has a fire pit, and you have a good supply of dry firewood (it must be dry; green wood will smoke and not burn hot enough), you can set out a grill over the fire and cook breakfast in an iron skillet. Or learn how to make a stew or bake a cake in a Dutch oven over the coals. The International Dutch Oven Society (www.idos.com) has lots of information on campfire cooking, cast-iron products, and links to recipes. Plus you'll find many campfire cooking books at Amazon.com or camping supply companies.

With a sun oven, you can cook delicious meals without using any fuel.
(Sun Ovens International)

Another alternative cooking method is a sun oven, which uses the sun to heat food to cooking temperature. One such product is the Global Sun Oven, which the manufacturer, Sun Ovens International, says will bake, boil, or steam any kind of food—no fuel needed. Go to www.sunoven.com for more information, including recipes. Although we've never used one, you may find it a useful option to check out.

Plan Ahead

Besides trying propane-free cooking methods, conserve your propane supply by doing some prep work at home—if you are not a fulltimer—before you leave. This will reduce cooking time when boondocking. Some ideas are:

- Cook meats such as ground beef or chicken. Season as you cook according to the meal. For example, season sliced chicken breasts Mexican style for chicken fajitas one night. Make sloppy joes at home and freeze. A little cooking to heat the meat, and you're all set.

- Cook breakfast sausages at home, slice, and freeze. Use them on your trip mixed in with scrambled eggs or onions and peppers.

- Cook a roast at home, slice, and freeze. Thaw later for sandwiches. Even add the gravy for hot roast beef sandwiches.

- Cook pasta at home to save water and propane. Mix in the sauce. Place in zip-top plastic bags. Store in the refrigerator or freezer and reheat as needed. (Mixing sauces into the pasta at home can be a space saver as well.)

STORING

Storage space being what it is on an RV—namely, probably less than you'd like—use your space wisely and look for ways to reduce bulk. Here are some ideas:

- Select food in packages that are impervious to humidity or drying out.

- Repackage foods in airtight containers. We transfer nearly all types of food except canned goods from the original packages to plastic containers with airtight lids.

- Choose containers that make the best use of each cabinet's storage space.

- Be sure all packages are insect- and vermin-proof.

GOOD FOOD, NEW FRIENDS, GREAT FUN

Good meals can definitely enhance your enjoyment of camping in isolated places. Bill does all the cooking in our RV. But he likes to say he doesn't do windows or dishes. He also loves to bake; he makes wonderful Danish pastries, pecan rolls, cakes, brownies, cookies, and other

Bill's Roast Beef Dinner

Bill likes to get one or two eye of round roasts that will fit in the pan. He cooks the roast(s) and vegetables together, so you'll need room for the veggies in the pan with the meat. Note: This recipe uses 3 hours of propane.

1. Preheat the oven to 350°F.
2. Completely trim any fat from the meat; season meat with salt and pepper.
3. Place the meat in a roasting pan and bake uncovered for 1 hour.
4. Remove the roast(s) from the oven.
5. To 1 cup water, add the following ingredients: 1 heaping teaspoon beef bouillon crystals (low sodium if available), salt, pepper, and $1/4$ cup red wine.
6. Pour this mixture over the meat, cover, and return to the oven for 2 hours.
7. While the meat is cooking, prepare the vegetables: peel and quarter 2 or 3 potatoes and slice $1/2$ onion and 1 or 2 carrots.
8. When the meat has about 40 minutes left to cook, add the vegetables to the roasting pan, and put the cover back on.
9. At the end of the cooking time, check that the vegetables are done, then remove them to a large dish.
10. Check the meat for tenderness by poking it several times with a fork. If you use a meat thermometer, it should read 190°F or higher.
11. Remove the meat to a platter, and make the gravy.

Many people seem to have a problem making good gravy. Here's Bill's method:

1. Dissolve 1 heaping tablespoon cornstarch in $1/4$ cup water; add more beef bouillon and wine to make $1/2$ cup.
2. Place the roasting pan on a burner and heat the pan juices until they start to bubble.
3. Add a little of the cornstarch mixture to the juices, stirring constantly.
4. As more bubbles appear, add more cornstarch mixture.
5. Repeat until the gravy is nice and thick.
6. Serve and enjoy!

delights such as lemon curd. We have also enjoyed many of Bill's roast beef dinners while we have been boondocking. Bill developed his roast beef recipe over several years, trying many different cuts of beef. He finally decided on eye of round as being the best cut for delicious tender meals and a great meat for sandwiches.

We found by chance, in a small drugstore, a nice little roasting pan with a lid that was perfect for fitting inside of our RV oven. These ovens are smaller than regular stove ovens and much searching will be necessary to find pans, cookie sheets, cake pans, and the like for use in RV cooking. The same is true for cooking dishes for the microwave and/or convection ovens, which are usually smaller than home appliances.

Getting together with fellow RVers is a great way to add to the fun of the boondocking and to make new friends. Usually, we all pitch in and come up with several

Our "New England" Boiled Dinner

This is a simple, tasty one-pan meal, which means less cleanup, and less water! You can make as much or as little as you like, depending on what you have on hand and how many people you want to feed.

1. Peel and chop the potatoes, carrots, and cabbage. Slice the sausage.
2. Put the vegetables and sausage in a pan with about $1/2$ inch of water. Salt and pepper the veggies.
3. Cover the pan and bring to a boil, then adjust the heat to simmer.
4. Cook until the potatoes are done, about 30 minutes.
5. Serve with plenty of butter and mustard.

good dishes for a potluck dinner. Once while we were at Quartzsite, we didn't know what to bring, until Jan remembered we had some sausage, cabbage, potatoes, and carrots, so we made a "New England" boiled dinner. It was a big hit.

In addition to potluck dinners, we've all had cookouts where we cooked hamburgers or hot dogs over a campfire. For many, especially kids, this can be the high spot of a boondocking weekend. Cooking and sharing meals not only add to the boondock camping experience, but create fun times and good memories. Perhaps you can collect recipes of some good baked bean dishes or chili for your next dry camping cookout, and don't forget to invite us!

CHAPTER 6

Heating and Cooling

K eeping the inside of your RV at a comfortable temperature can be a challenge when boondocking. Both air conditioners and furnaces consume large amounts of power. An air conditioner requires a generator, and an electrical furnace will probably require more power than your batteries can handle over a long period. Even though your furnace burns propane, the fan and thermostat are electrically powered and will consume 12-volt battery power. However, there are ways of keeping your RV heated and cooled, which we'll cover in this chapter.

(RVIA)

HEATING

You can stay warm with several types of propane heaters that do not require electrical power. These include catalytic and open-flame heaters.

We have used both types for over twenty years, and neither of us has suffered from their use. When using a propane heater, you can take specific measures to help you stay safe and healthy:

■ Provide adequate ventilation. It is very important to have sufficient ventilation in your RV when operating a propane heater. Depending upon the heater (discussed later), too little ventilation can result in either oxygen depletion or carbon monoxide poisoning. Read your heater's instructions for proper ventilation.

Keep in mind, too, that most RV windows are not airtight, unless they are dual-pane windows, because they usually have small vents in the frame to control condensation. With the number of windows in the average RV, there is a considerable amount of air constantly moving through the rig, which alone might be enough. However, we also always keep the stove vent propped open by using a spring clip to hold the outside flapper up. We also keep a roof vent open about an inch or so.

■ Install a carbon monoxide detector. Carbon monoxide (CO) is a deadly gas and a detector will alarm if harmful CO levels occur. Also be aware of the signs and symptoms of carbon monoxide poisoning (see the sidebar on page 50).

■ Periodically check propane gas lines for leaks, and have them inspected annually by a professional.

■ Follow manufacturer's instructions as to placement and distance from flammable objects.

Catalytic Heaters

Catalytic heaters are ventless propane heaters that require no electricity for operation. They work by using a catalyst—a platinum-impregnated pad—that produces heat when combined with oxygen and propane. The result is a flameless heat that ranges from 1,600 to 8,000 Btu. They can be either wall mounted or portable.

These heaters have two settings: high and low. They do not have thermostats, so will not turn off unless you turn them off. The largest catalytic heater on the high setting can consume almost as much propane as the average furnace, so keep an eye on your propane use when boondocking.

While a catalytic heater burns oxygen, it does not have an open flame. It produces a radiant heat that heats a specific object, such as a couch or chair, rather than the air. The intense heat can scorch cabinets and walls, and perhaps even start a fire, if the heater is placed within 3 feet of such objects. As a precaution, we made and installed "barn doors" (see the photo below) on either side of the portable heater so the heat is directed away from flammable areas.

The doors were cut from a piece of aluminum by a sheet metal shop and bent to our specifications. We drilled holes in each piece, pop-riveted the hinges to the doors, and added a mounting strip. Then we installed the hinges and doors on the heater with very short screws.

We have two catalytic heaters—a small one (1,600 to 2,800 Btu), which is mounted on the wall, and a medium-sized one (3,200 to 6,000 Btu) we can move around as needed. We've kept warm in some below-freezing temperatures with the catalytic heaters as our only heat source. In mild weather, the small heater is adequate, but in consistently colder weather, we use the larger heater. In especially cold weather, we've used both heaters, connecting the portable unit to the gas line at the mounted heater using a flexible gas hose running off a flared T-fitting (for more, see page 51).

Our catalytic propane heater with the folding doors that we made to protect the cabinetry near it.

Staying Safe: Catalytic Heaters

As noted, a catalytic heater consumes oxygen to burn. The danger with this is that in an enclosed space with poor ventilation, it can deplete the oxygen in the air. This can cause hypoxia, which is a medical condition that occurs when the body doesn't get enough oxygen. It produces similar symptoms as CO poisoning, namely, headaches, fatigue, shortness of breath, and nausea. Severe hypoxia can cause unconsciousness and death.

An additional hazard is the buildup of CO. When there is enough oxygen in the air, a catalytic heater burns very cleanly, producing only water and carbon dioxide as by-products. However, as with any combustion process, as the oxygen level drops, combustion becomes incomplete and CO results.

The combination of low oxygen levels and the presence of CO results in an unhealthy and potentially dangerous atmosphere.

The solution is simple but important: provide adequate ventilation to keep the oxygen in the air at safe levels for both people and heaters. Follow the manufacturer's instructions for what defines adequate ventilation.

Note: Some catalytic heaters come with an oxygen depletion sensor (see opposite) that alarms and shuts off the heater when the oxygen in the air drops to an unsafe level. And as noted earlier, a CO detector monitors CO levels.

In those rare cases, where we have had below-zero temperatures, we have used both heaters as well as the furnace.

One disadvantage with a catalytic heater is that over time the pad can become contaminated. If it does, you must replace it, and the pads are quite expensive. Contaminants include room deodorant sprays, water in the propane, dust, and dirt. You can purchase a dust cover for some heater models, which may help protect the pad when the heater is not in use.

A blue-flame heater mounted on the end of the sink counter.

Open-Flame Heaters

The other types of propane heaters that we are seeing more frequently in RVs are ceramic and blue-flame heaters.

Ceramic heaters use a small flame to heat a ceramic disc(s) to a high temperature; the disc in turn radiates the heat into the room. The flame can be either manually adjusted or regulated with a thermostat. Blue-flame heaters show a blue flame along the length of a burner. They also can be either manually adjusted or thermostatically controlled so that the unit turns the flame on and off as the temperature varies.

These heaters have two advantages over catalytic heaters: (1) they produce a higher Btu rating—10,000 to 20,000, and (2) they have no pad you have to replace. The disadvantage of both is that they are ventless heaters, which means that fumes stay in the space where the heaters are located.

We have friends who use both types of heaters and are very happy with them, primarily because they produce a higher Btu rating than catalytic heaters. We recently installed a blue-flame heater and like it very much. Maintenance is easy; we just vacuum the dust occasionally.

Oxygen Depletion Sensors

Some catalytic and ceramic heaters come with oxygen depletion sensors that monitor the level of oxygen and shut off the heater if that level drops below a safe point. Consequently, these heaters may not work above certain elevations because the oxygen levels drop below the sensors' shutoff point.

Unfortunately, these altitudes eliminate most of the American West, places where most RVers wish to travel. If you plan to camp at these higher altitudes, discuss this issue with your dealer to find the safest heater for the altitudes you'll be at.

Staying Safe: Carbon Monoxide

Carbon monoxide (CO) is an odorless, colorless gas that can cause symptoms from a mild headache to death. CO is a by-product of combustion. Your car engine produces it, as do gas generators and propane heaters and stoves. It is important to take CO emissions seriously, be aware of their health symptoms, and take preventive measures to control and detect CO.

Carbon monoxide enters your bloodstream through your lungs and binds with the hemoglobin molecules in your blood that carry oxygen throughout the body. The danger comes from the fact that CO binds quicker to hemoglobin than oxygen, thus displacing the oxygen. This decreases the amount of oxygen getting to your body's tissues and vital organs (i.e., your heart, lungs, and brain). The more CO you inhale, the less oxygen your body gets and the more severe your symptoms will be.

The symptoms of CO poisoning depend on how much CO is in the air, how long you are exposed to it, and your general state of health. Initial symptoms include:

- Tightness across the chest
- Headache
- Fatigue
- Dizziness
- Drowsiness
- Nausea
- Sudden chest pain in people with angina

Prolonged exposure or higher concentrations of CO cause increasingly severe symptoms:

- Vomiting
- Confusion
- Collapse
- Loss of consciousness
- Muscle weakness
- Death

Some people are more susceptible to CO poisoning: infants, children, and the elderly; anyone with heart or lung diseases or anemia; and smokers, who already have CO in their bloodstream from cigarettes. CO poisoning poses a special risk to fetuses. Also if you are camping at a high altitude, where there is a lower level of oxygen in the air, you may feel the effects of CO sooner.

If you or your family members feel you are experiencing symptoms of CO poisoning, leave the RV and get to fresh air. Contact the fire department or local emergency services and also seek medical attention for a proper diagnosis. Have your propane appliances checked before reentering the RV.

However, since CO is odorless and colorless, you may be incapacitated before you can request assistance. The best way to prevent CO poisoning is to install a CO detector, which detects the presence of CO and sets off an alarm when levels reach a preset point. Be sure to buy one that meets the requirements of the current Underwriters Laboratory (UL) standard 2034 or the International Approval Services (IAS) 6-96 standard. CO detectors that withstand vibration shock, humidity, cooking fumes, and temperature extremes are available specifically for RVs.

If your alarm goes off, The American Red Cross (www.redcross.org) advises the following: Treat the alarm as a real emergency. If it sounds and you don't have any symptoms, press the reset button. (If you do have symptoms, leave the RV immediately.) If it sounds again, call the fire department and have your system checked to determine why the alarm continues to sound.

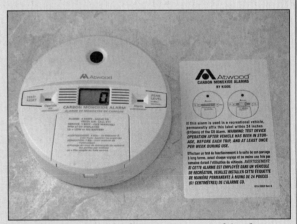

A carbon monoxide detector mounted in the bedroom for protection.

Connecting a Propane Heater

If you decide to connect a propane heater to a gas line, call in a professional. He or she should only use pipe fittings or flared fittings, **not** compression-type fittings. Compression fittings, which are the small brass rings used on many appliances, can leak propane. The installer must use a flared fitting on copper tubing. We recommend first installing a good-quality, large-handled shutoff valve in the $^3/_8$-inch copper tubing, then placing a flared brass T-fitting next to the heater. The unused side of the T-fitting should be capped so it won't leak. Later if it gets really cold you can place another heater, equipped with feet, on the unused side of the T-fitting by using a gas hose.

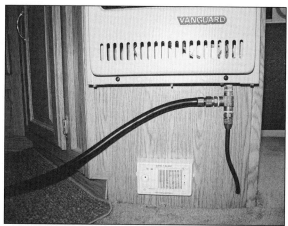

A propane hose and T-fitting connecting two propane heaters to one gas connection.

One final note: Government agencies, both federal and state, have made a mess with laws and requirements concerning the heaters discussed in this chapter. One of the worst things that produces carbon monoxide is the good old cookstove, particularly the oven. Yet all these agencies have given their seal of approval to these appliances. Nothing is mentioned about the need for ventilation.

We have used these appliances without harm. As mentioned, catalytic heaters, which are ventless, do use up the oxygen in the air, so ventilation is necessary. Open-flame heaters are also ventless and additionally produce carbon monoxide. We have had a blue-flame heater for six years now and have used it almost continuously during the winter without problems. We must strongly stress, however, that the decision to use any of the propane heaters we have described in this chapter must be made by you. You must assume the responsibility for your own safety. (Note: Some people do not like or tolerate the smell of burning propane. It can make their eyes tear and cause nausea. These people should not use propane appliances.)

Propane is a very safe fuel to use and burns cleaner than diesel or gasoline. The solution to using any propane product safely is, as we've said, ventilation: open a window, stove vent, and/or a roof vent. And install a carbon monoxide detector in the bedroom area.

COOLING

As important as heating is, it is far more likely the average boondocker will be more concerned with cooling his or her RV. Air conditioners are not a good option for boondocking (unless you have a generator of at least 4,000 watts), and can have their own CO problems, so we won't cover them in this book. We will, however, cover fans, swamp coolers, and window coverings as ways to keep the inside of your RV cool and comfortable.

Fans

There are several types of fans for RVs. For starters, a roof vent fan is a great choice for removing warm air from an RV—and we're not talking about the dinky little fan found on the vent over the shower in many RVs. Rather, we mean a fan with blades large enough to fill the vent. One popular vent fan is the Fan-tastic Vent (www.fantas ticvent.com).

A Fan-tastic vent fan is a great way to cool your RV.

The Fan-tastic vent fan uses a small amount of 12-volt power, about 2.2 amps on low speed, and can move a lot of air. We often find it moves enough air through the trailer to keep it quite comfortable when the outside temperature is in the eighties. Since the heat of the day is usually in the late afternoon, our solar panels are able to keep up with the amperage draw of the fan.

Another fan option is a small 12-volt fan. Mount one on a wall or make it portable by fastening it to a small board. Then you can place it where you need it, plugging it into a nearby 12-volt outlet. We even suggest you place one on the wall over the foot of your bed to keep you cool on a hot night. This type of fan draws very little amperage.

You can also run small portable AC fans, either box type or oscillating type, off an inverter if their wattage is not too high.

Once several years ago, while visiting an RV show and walking through a fifth-wheeler, Bill came out of the bedroom and was almost decapitated by an overhead ceiling fan. At the time we thought putting a large ceiling fan in an RV was a rather stupid idea. However, when we later bought a trailer with a ceiling fan already installed, we found out how useful one could be. While most of them are low-wattage AC units, we understand several models are offered in 12-volt DC versions. They can cool the whole RV on moderately warm days.

Swamp Coolers

Another type of air cooler is an evaporative cooler, more commonly called a swamp cooler. Swamp coolers work best in a low-humidity location, such as the desert areas of the West. Warm, dry air is pulled into the cooler and pushed through a wet filter, where it picks up moisture. As the moisture evaporates, it cools the air. Several factors can affect the efficiency of swamp coolers; e.g., relative humidity, air temperature, the size of the RV, and how well the RV is insulated.

There are several brands and models of evaporative coolers on the market. Some are portable and run on 12-volt DC; other larger models run on 120-volt AC. If you are old enough to remember way back before automobile air conditioners came into use, people used to mount a similar type of cooler in their car window. Most of the 12-volt models are small portable units measuring from 7 by 12 by 12 inches to 14 by 12 by 12 inches. They not only cool the interior of an RV but function as a high-capacity fan as well. The nice thing about these units is that they draw only about 4.2 amps on the low setting to about 13.9 amps on the high setting. This low setting is low enough that solar panels could probably operate the cooler during the day, as long as the batteries were not too badly discharged the night before. Swamp coolers will also run on a small portable generator, making them very practical. They cost considerably less than a regular RV air conditioner.

One swamp cooler made specifically for RVs is the TurboKOOL Evaporative Air Cooler (www.turbokool.com). It fits in the standard 14-by-14-inch roof vent on your RV and runs on 12 volts (amperage draw is 4.6 amps on the high setting, 3.2 amps on medium, and 2.2 amps on low). The TurboKOOL will cool 750 cubic feet per minute (cfm) on high and 450 cfm on low, which will very nicely cool a 21-foot, fifth-wheel trailer. Larger RVs would require two or more units. When installing, you can connect the cooler to the RV's water system so the water reservoir is filled automatically, or you can fill it via a hose. As an added feature, the unit has a filtration system that will remove dust, pollen, and impurities from the air.

Keep in mind that the lower the humidity in the air, the colder the air temperature will be as the air exits the cooler. Bachman Enterprises, the manufacturer of the TurboKOOL, states that the average relative humidity should not exceed 75%. (Other swamp cooler manufacturers say they will still cool in high-humidity places, only not as well.) See the efficiency chart supplied by TurboKOOL that compares the outside temperature to the cooled inside temperature.

TurboKOOL® Efficiency Temperature Output
Fahrenheit

Outside Air Temperature F	2	5	10	15	20	25	30	35	40	45	50	55	60	65	70	75	80
125	83	86	90	93	96												
120	81	83	86	90	93	95											
115	78	80	83	86	89	91	94										
110	75	77	80	83	85	87	90	92									
105	72	74	77	79	81	84	86	88	89								
100	69	71	73	76	78	80	82	83	85	87	88						
95	67	68	70	72	74	76	78	79	81	82	84	85	87				
90	64	65	67	69	70	72	74	76	77	78	79	81	82	83	84	86	
85	61	62	63	65	67	68	70	71	72	73	74	75	76	77	79	81	
80	57	58	60	62	63	64	66	67	68	69	71	72	73	74	76	76	77
75	54	55	57	58	59	61	62	63	64	65	66	67	68	69	70	71	72

% Relative Humidity

TurboKOOL® Efficiency Temperature Output
Celsius

Outside Air Temperature C	2	5	10	15	20	25	30	35	40	45	50	55	60	65	70	75	80
52	28	30	32	34	36												
49	27	28	30	32	34	35											
46	26	27	28	30	32	33	34										
43	24	25	27	28	29	31	32	33									
41	22	23	25	26	27	29	30	31	32								
38	21	22	23	24	26	27	28	28	29	31	31						
35	19	20	21	22	23	24	26	26	27	28	29	29	31				
32	18	18	19	21	21	22	23	24	25	26	26	27	28	28	29	30	
29	16	17	17	18	19	20	21	22	22	23	23	24	24	25	26	27	
27	14	14	16	17	17	18	19	19	20	21	22	22	23	23	24	24	25
24	12	13	14	14	15	16	17	17	18	18	19	19	20	21	21	22	22

% Relative Humidity

This chart shows how much cooling an evaporative cooler will do in various outside temperatures and humidity. For instance, at 110°F and 30% humidity the cooler would lower the temperature 20°. (Bachman Enterprises)

A TurboKOOL cooler mounted on the roof of an RV. (RVIA)

We personally have not had any experience with swamp coolers, but we do think they might be a good substitute for an air conditioner if you spend most of your time in the desert areas of the West.

Window Coverings

The window coverings in your RV can help keep you cool. Some pleated shades have an insulating feature, as do good-quality, light-blocking, roller-type window shades. In the summertime, these are effective for keeping the sun out (and in the winter, they'll help keep the heat in). Miniblinds do not have these properties. Dual-pane windows also contribute to keeping your interior cool in the summer and warm in the winter, although they are expensive and must be ordered from the manufacturer at the time you buy your rig.

An awning that runs the length of the RV or individual awnings on each window will shade the RV and keep it cooler. Some of the newer models unfurl themselves at the push of a button and will roll themselves up if the wind gets too strong.

CHAPTER 7

Communications and Navigation

As mentioned in Chapter 1, boondocking doesn't mean leaving the world behind—unless, of course, that's what you want. New developments in the fields of computers and communications provide direct benefits for the boondocking RVer.

CELL PHONES

Cell phones have not only become a great convenience, but we believe a real necessity for RVers for reasons of time, money, and safety. Many cell-phone plans include unlimited long-distance service with no roaming charges, and coverage areas are broader than ever before. In fact, coverage today is almost 100% along interstate highways, so if you have an emergency you can reach help instantly.

(RVIA)

Recently Bill was traveling alone in our rig just outside a very small town in Idaho when he blew a tire on the trailer. He tried but couldn't reach our emergency road service or anyone else on the cell phone. Since the tire blew on a curve while going up a hill, he reasoned that the trees and the hill were affecting the phone's signal strength. So he started walking down the hill toward the town about 2 miles away. Eventually he got a weak signal just around the bend and was able to call our emergency road service. Because he was on a small intermediary highway, it took over 2 hours for help to arrive, but it did come eventually. The driver swapped the blown tire for the spare in short order, and Bill drove to Moscow, Idaho, 20 miles back down the road where he could buy a new tire and get back on the road.

A few years ago, this situation would not have been resolved so easily and conveniently (even with the wait). You would have had to unhitch the tow vehicle, drive back to find help to change the tire, rehitch, and go to a tire dealer for a new tire.

Digital cell phones operate between 0.25 and 0.6 watt, with a range of about 20 to 30 miles. A booster, such as the SmoothTalker (www.smoothtalker.com), can raise that output to 3 watts, the wattage at which analog cell phones operated (and they always had great range). This results in a signal five times stronger than the phone's original signal.

We know of many campgrounds, for both boondocking and regular RVing, that we would like to visit but hesitate to do so for long-term stays because of poor cell-phone coverage. With a booster, these places are more accessible.

SmoothTalker claims that in flat country and under optimum conditions, its units can transmit a signal up to 60 miles. A more realistic distance is probably about 30 to 40 miles in average terrain, which is still pretty good. The only obstacles that can stop or interfere with the signal are hills, trees, and buildings.

Even wattage-boosting antennas can help improve your cell-phone signal, particularly when you are calling from inside your rig. The reason is that most trailers and motorhomes are basically metal cages—consisting of steel or aluminum frames. Both of these metals are great signal stoppers. Outside antennas on a rig can be a big help, whether they are roof mounted or window mounted using a through-the-glass type of antenna. (An antenna will work on dual-pane windows, but not as well as the magnetic-type antennas used on the roof.)

When you are boondocking, any technique or technology that will improve your ability to communicate with the outside world is worth the peace of mind. You never know when you may have a medical emergency, so it is nice to know you can summon help when you need it. If your cell phone has a GPS receiver installed, when you call 911, it will transmit your exact position in latitude and longitude to the 911 operator. This feature is the reason why so many people trapped or lost in out-of-the-way places are successfully rescued.

E-MAIL

Most RVers use e-mail to stay in touch with relatives, RVing friends, and even business contacts. For years, we've used PocketMail (www.pocketmail.com) for our e-mail, which is a mobile e-mail service that uses a telephone to transmit your messages. We can easily correspond weekly with family and certain friends.

The PocketMail Composer is a small handheld device with a keyboard and LCD screen. You compose your e-mail messages using the keyboard, then transmit the messages with a telephone. The unit has a fold-out microphone and a receiver, and the whole thing fits neatly over a telephone receiver. Dial the PocketMail service, and when it answers, hold the unit up to the receiver and push the send button. PocketMail also has a device you can connect to a PDA, giving you mobile e-mail.

Today, we find that with the ever-increasing disappearance of pay phones and the development of other better computer methods, we use PocketMail less and less.

INTERNET ACCESS

When you're home or in a private campground with complete facilities, you have many options for accessing the Internet:

- Dial-up: uses your computer's built-in, dial-up modem, a phone line, a telephone cable with an RJ-11 jack on each end, and an account with an Internet service provider (ISP).

- Broadband: a high-speed connection, with two options—DSL (digital subscriber line), which uses a special phone line; or cable and the same RG-59 coaxial cable used for television reception.

- Wi-fi: short for *wi*reless *fi*delity; uses small radio transceivers built into the computer or in a PC card to send and receive the signals between the host and your computer. The problem with wi-fi is range, which is only 100 to 150 feet indoors.

- Cell phone: uses a cell phone—see below.

- PC card for a cell-phone tower: uses a specific PC card from your cell-phone provider; see below.

- Internet satellite dish: allows access to a satellite for Internet service (separate from a television satellite dish); see below.

When you're boondocking, however, the only viable options for accessing the Internet are cell phones, a PC card for cell-phone towers, and an Internet satellite dish, all of which we cover below.

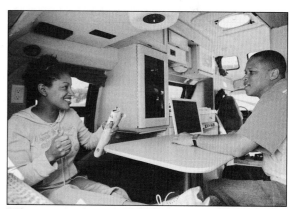

When you're boondocking, you can still keep up with current events by accessing the Internet on your laptop. (RVIA)

Cell-Phone Access

New technology now allows you to use your cell phone to access the Internet from your laptop computer. We have used Verizon's mobile-office kit for about four years now and have found it to be satisfactory—within reason. With a transfer speed of only 14.4 kilobytes per second, it is awfully slow, plus we have to be in range of a cell-phone tower. We've also tried Verizon's broadband service, which is faster and works very well. However, it is also expensive, and we still need to be in range of a cell tower.

If you want to use your cell phone for the Internet, make sure you have a phone with the necessary features, matching software, and a connecting cord. Many phones are not suited for this purpose.

PC Cards and Cell-Phone Towers

You can also use a cell-phone tower to access the Internet from your laptop in the same way your cell phone works. All you need is a PC card provided by your cell-phone company that plugs into the PC slot on your computer. The service is broadband, with data transmitted over radio waves. The card has its own antenna and cell-phone number, and it will not affect your regular cell-phone use. We find this system works well for us.

The one drawback is you're still limited to a 5- to 7-mile range from the nearest cell-phone tower. However, as with a cell phone, you can use a booster or amplifier to increase that range. You can purchase cables that will fit most cards, as well as antennas to fit on your RV. Check with SmoothTalker about its units.

Our computer setup. Not shown is the floppy disk drive or the DVD and CD burner drive.

Internet Satellite Dishes

All RVers are familiar with satellite dishes and the wonderful TV service they provide. It seems that most RVs nowadays are equipped with one, whether it is a portable or roof-mounted unit. A new development that has appeared on the scene is the Internet satellite dish. These dishes come as either a tripod-mounted dish, which must be manually aligned to the satellite, or a roof-mounted unit that automatically adjusts with the push of a button. Either way you go, this technology is probably the best solution for boondockers wishing to get on the Internet.

The systems are expensive though; the roof-mounted automatic dishes run from $5,000 to $6,000 (installation is extra), and the manual tripod dishes range from $1,300 to $1,500 dollars.

Internet satellite dishes are much more sensitive to alignment than television dishes, although once aligned, they work well. With the manual dishes, you will have to devote a certain amount of time to learning how to find the satellite. While we've had no experience with either type, we have heard that the tripod models are very difficult to align with the correct satellite. Plus it can be a real chore to realign the dish every day while traveling. A friend who has a roof-mounted model says he is very happy with his because it is so easy to use.

The tripod dishes are also much larger than the television ones, so storing a unit while you travel may pose a problem.

SATELLITE RADIO

One form of satellite communication that we enjoy very much is satellite radio. At present there are two companies offering programming, XM Radio and Sirius. Both companies broadcast all kinds of music on many channels: pop, rock, blues, hip-hop, swing, country, bluegrass, jazz, classical, and some other types we have probably forgotten to mention. They also offer news, weather, talk shows, politics, and sports (with many sports events covered from kickoff to the last inning). Recently, we were given an XM Radio receiver and we enjoyed it immensely during a trip to Arizona. We never had to worry about switching stations when a signal started fading out. Satellite radio is ideal for boondockers—especially when we are camping in areas with no radio coverage and thus no local access to news and weather.

GLOBAL POSITIONING SYSTEM (GPS) RECEIVERS

GPS is a twenty-four-satellite navigational system that was developed by the U.S. Department of Defense for military use. However, because of the system's enormous potential, the government released it for civilian purposes in the 1980s.

GPS works in any weather, anywhere in the world, 24 hours a day. The GPS satellites are in very precise orbits and emit radio signal information as they circle the earth. GPS receivers lock onto these satellite signals and measure the time delay it takes for the radio signal to reach the receiver. A receiver must lock onto at least three satellites to pinpoint its actual latitude and longitude. With four or more satellites, it can also calculate altitude. The accuracy is within just a few feet. Other available information includes speed, bearing, trip distance, and destination distance.

GPS receivers range in size from small handheld units to larger ones that can be mounted on the dashboard of your tow vehicle or motorhome, and they range in price from $100 to over $1,000. You can also attach a unit to your laptop and use mapping software. When programmed, a receiver can follow a course from one end of the country to the other, giving audio driving instructions to guide you along the way. The viewing screen displays a full-color, graphic map of all the turns, highway changes, and service stations along the way, even the nearest McDonald's, until it finally puts you in your destination campground. GPS receivers are so sensitive they can also guide you up a four-wheel trail in the mountains, showing every turn. The single RVer can get a lot of help with his or her navigation with one of these great devices.

CHAPTER 8

Boondock Electricity Made Easy

The biggest problem a boondock RVer confronts is the one of charging the RV's batteries rapidly and completely enough after a night without an electrical hookup. This is particularly true when the RVer wants to boondock for several nights in succession before moving on. The folks at *Trailer Life* magazine told us quite a few years ago that one of their most frequently asked questions was, "How do you charge the house batteries in the RV after boondocking?" (We'll draw the distinction between house batteries and starting batteries shortly.)

We believe many RVers would like to do more boondock camping, but upon trying it they are stymied by depleted batteries that they can't seem to recharge. Consequently they

(Winnebago Industries)

don't try primitive camping again. But the rewards of boondock camping are too great to let this scare you away. Dead batteries may be an inconvenience, but they're nothing to fear. The world won't come to an end if your batteries die. Practice electricity conservation, match your battery capacity to your needs or your needs to your capacity, and recharge your batteries as soon and as thoroughly as possible, and you'll do fine.

Another problem is that many people are afraid of electricity, thinking that it requires esoteric knowledge and higher math. Fearing that any electrical system modifications they make in their RVs could have unforeseen consequences, they avoid the subject altogether.

The truth of the matter is that the electrical knowledge the average RVer needs for boondocking is very small and can be learned quickly. All things electrical are interrelated. Once the fundamental relations are grasped, the electrical system as a whole is easy to understand.

BASIC BOONDOCKING

Many people practice basic boondocking without even thinking about it. They will pull into a place, spend the night, then move on the next morning, recharging the batteries through their alternator as they drive down the road. This is easy to do, and is probably the simplest form of boondocking.

Many of today's alternators, however, are only designed to replace the current used to start the engine, not to replenish partial or fully discharged batteries. This is particularly true with the alternators on many trucks, SUVs, and passenger cars. The alternator's amperage output is just high enough to replace the current used to start the engine, and then the current tapers off rapidly until it has very little charging capability.

While it's true that a starting motor places a heavy draw on a battery, that demand lasts no more than a few seconds. In contrast, the demands placed on a battery by "house" needs—lights, fans, refrigerator, coffeemaker, computer, TV, etc.—have the capacity to discharge a battery much more deeply over time than a starting motor ever does. The crux of the boondock RVer's problem is to have enough battery capacity to meet domestic needs when not plugged into a campground outlet, and enough charging capacity to replenish those batteries efficiently.

YOUR RV'S ELECTRICAL SYSTEM

An RV has all the normal automotive electrical needs, of course—headlights, dashboard lights, power windows, radio, and so on—but since these are only needed when the engine is running, supplying them with power is not a problem. The standard automotive battery and alternator are so good at satisfying these needs that you rarely even have to think about them.

But your RV also needs to supply power for cooking, recreation, communication, creature comforts, and other domestic needs when the engine isn't running, and this is a taller order to fill. Your RV's "house" electrical system comprises both DC (direct current—i.e., battery-supplied) and AC (alternating or household current) appliances. DC appliances

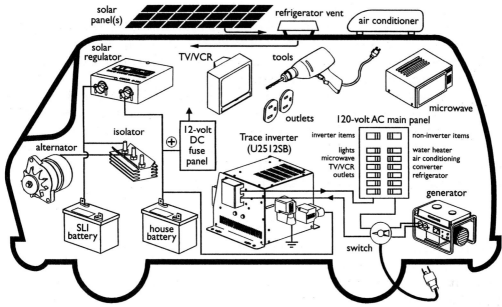

solar panel(s)
refrigerator vent
air conditioner
solar regulator
TV/VCR
tools
microwave
isolator
12-volt DC fuse panel
Trace inverter (U2512SB)
120-volt AC main panel
alternator
outlets
inverter items
non-inverter items
lights
microwave
TV/VCR
outlets
water heater
air conditioning
converter
refrigerator
generator
SLI battery
house battery
switch

Components of an RV electrical system. (Xantrex)

include 12-volt lights, the freshwater pump, and perhaps the furnace, among other conveniences. AC appliances include fluorescent lights, a satellite dish, a television, a DVD/VCR, a laptop computer, a microwave, and small kitchen appliances such as a coffeemaker—unless, of course, you have 12-volt versions of any of these.

When you're boondocking, all these appliances are powered by your batteries, either directly in the case of DC appliances or through a DC/AC inverter in the case of AC appliances. Yes, you could generate AC power from a gasoline or diesel generator—either a small portable one or a larger installed unit—but generators have decided drawbacks as we'll see in Chapter 11.

Our preferred approach is to manage our electrical needs carefully, carry enough battery capacity to meet those needs, monitor our battery usage and recharging closely, and meet as much of our electrical needs as possible with solar panels. This is the approach we will be describing in this and the following chapters. If you're thinking about boondock RVing, think twice before buying an RV that is laden with power-hungry AC appliances. Our refrigerator operates on either AC power or propane, and we use a gas oven rather than an AC convection oven.

BATTERY BASICS

Let's start our discussion of batteries by considering the starting battery you find in any automobile. The standard automotive starting battery is a 12-volt wet-cell lead-acid battery—also known as a flooded-electrolyte or liquid-electrolyte battery—composed of six cells, with each cell having a potential when fully charged of 2.105 volts. Thus, the voltage of a fully charged automotive battery is $6 \times 2.105 = 12.63$ volts.

Each battery cell contains an odd number of lead plates that are either positively or negatively charged. These plates look like a grid with rectangular holes. The grid holds the material that will provide the electrons with which the battery generates power. Positive plates contain a lead dioxide paste; negative plates contain sponge lead. These plates are immersed in a solution of 25% sulfuric acid and water, which acts as the electrolyte (a solution that allows electric current to flow through it). The positive plates are connected to each other and to the positive terminal of the battery; the negative plates are connected to each other and to the negative terminal. A battery has one more negative plate than positive. Between the plates are nonconducting insulators, called separators, that prevent the negative and positive plates from touching and thus short-circuiting.

When you use the energy stored in the battery, a chemical reaction occurs. The acid reacts with the materials in the plates, producing lead sulfate and water, which dilutes the sulfuric acid solution. As the reaction continues, the voltage potential of the battery decreases. Once the electrolyte becomes mostly pure water, the battery is fully discharged.

When you recharge a battery, you reverse this process. The water and lead sulfate are

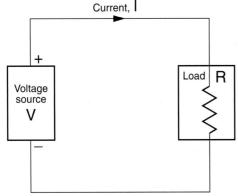

A simple electrical circuit. (Reprinted with permission from *Boatowner's Illustrated Electrical Handbook,* second edition, by Charlie Wing)

Volts, Amps, and Circuits

It's useful to compare electricity flowing through a copper wire to water flowing through a common garden hose. The voltage potential that causes the flow of electricity is analogous to the water main pressure maintained by your city's public works department, except that electrical pressure is measured in volts rather than pounds. And the resultant rate of electrical flow through the wire is analogous to the rate of water flow through the hose except that it's measured in amperes instead of gallons per minute. Water flows in only one direction, as does direct current (DC) electrical power supplied from a battery or a converter. The analogy breaks down somewhat with alternating current (AC) power, which flows in both directions along a wire, first in one phase and then the other. AC power (like the 110- or 220-volt power in a house) is supplied from a campground hookup, a generator, or from a battery via an inverter.

In order to produce some form of productive work, all electricity must travel in a complete circle, going from the voltage source (the batteries when you're boondocking) to the appliance or load and back to the source again. This completes a *circuit* (see illustration at left).

Electricity is also *polarized,* with a positive, or plus, side, and a negative, or minus, side. Therefore, most electrical circuits require two wires—one positive and one negative. The positive wire goes from the source of power to the appliance, and the negative wire returns to the source.

converted back to lead and lead dioxide, and the electrolyte solution increases in strength as the water is removed.

During discharging, the acid must remain in contact with the lead for the process to continue. To achieve this, the lead materials are porous so the acid can diffuse through the plates. This allows the water to move out and fresh acid to move in (much as tea diffuses through the filter material in a tea bag when you're making a cup of tea). The reverse happens during charging.

The rate at which this occurs is called the *diffusion rate*, and it can vary. The electrolyte reacts quickly with the surface areas of the plates. But as these areas are discharged, the acid must now diffuse into the inner plates, and this happens more slowly.

For example, when you try to start an engine on a very cold morning, the battery operates the starter for only a short time and then seems to go dead. If you let the battery rest, it revives. The reason is that you've given the acid time to diffuse into the inner plates. Diffusion is also the reason for a battery's slow acceptance of a charge during the recharging process. The surface areas of the plates receive their charge quickly, but it takes time for the electrolyte to reach the inner plates. The rate at which this occurs is the battery's *charge acceptance rate*.

Cutaway view of a battery. (Trojan Battery Company)

A Few Electrical Terms

Most people have heard electrical terms and may even use them, but here are a few definitions for clarity:

- **ampere (A), or amp:** the unit of measure for the flow rate of electric current
- **ampere-hour (Ah), or amp-hour:** a measure of the quantity of current that has flowed over time; a current of 7 amps flowing for 3 hours would draw 21 amp-hours of electricity from a battery
- **current (I):** the flow of electrons through a material (measured in amperes)
- **resistance:** opposition to electric current (measured in ohms); a voltage drop of 1 volt across a device through which 1 ampere of current is flowing means a resistance of 1 ohm; a voltage drop of 6 volts across a device through which 2 amperes of current is flowing means a resistance of 3 ohms
- **voltage (V):** the force that pushes current through a circuit
- **voltage drop:** the loss of voltage between one point in a circuit and another caused by resistance
- **watt (W):** the unit of electrical power; watts = volts x amps; a 12-volt light drawing 1 amp is consuming 12 watts of power

Gassing

During the recharging process, the water is broken down into hydrogen and oxygen, which are released as gases, resulting in the loss of electrolyte. With every discharge and recharge cycle, the battery loses more electrolyte. Checking the level of electrolyte is a standard maintenance task for wet-cell batteries (we'll cover maintenance at the end of this chapter). If the level is low, add **only** distilled water; **do not** use tap or rainwater since they can contain minerals that will damage the battery.

You can also mitigate electrolyte loss by replacing the regular vent caps with special caps called Hydrocaps. These allow the hydrogen and oxygen gases to recombine to water, and the water returns to the cell. Hydrocaps require regular maintenance; if they get dirty and become plugged, the result can be disastrous.

Shedding

Shedding is a natural outcome of charging and recharging a battery. Over time, the bond between the lead materials and the grid is weakened, and some material falls off and accumulates at the bottom of the battery. As more and more material falls off, the *battery capacity* (the amount of energy the battery can store) diminishes because the battery has less material with which to supply the chemical reaction.

Shedding is part of a battery's aging process and cannot be fixed. Eventually, one of two things will happen: (1) the battery will lose so much lead material that the chemical process can no longer occur, or (2) enough material will accumulate on the bottom of the battery to reach the plates and short-circuit the battery. Either way, the battery fails.

Sulfation

As we learned above, lead sulfate forms during discharging and converts back to lead and lead dioxide during charging. Lead sulfate is normally a soft material and easily reconverted. Under certain conditions, however, the soft lead sulfate hardens into crystals and is no longer able to reconvert. This phenomenon is called *sulfation*, and it will shorten the life of your battery.

Sulfation occurs under these conditions:

- The battery is left in a discharged state for a long period of time.
- The battery is consistently undercharged, leaving part of the battery uncharged and in the lead sulfate state.
- The inner areas of a battery's thick plates are not charged (a variant of undercharging).
- The battery self-discharges because it has not been used.

To prevent sulfation, ensure that your battery is properly and completely charged after each discharge cycle.

Self-Discharging

A fully charged wet-cell battery, when it is left idle with no charging and recharging cycles, will self-discharge over time. This is due to electrochemical processes within the battery, equivalent to the application of a small external load.

Overcharging

As we just covered, the charging process coverts water and lead sulfate back to lead and lead dioxide. If a battery is overcharged, the lead is converted to lead oxide, which is basically a nonconductive material. With this loss of conductive material, both the battery's capacity and acceptance rate are reduced. In effect, you'll get less power from the battery and a shorter life span.

Additionally, overcharging increases gassing of the electrolyte. This produces more oxygen and hydrogen gases, which increase the danger of a battery explosion.

TYPES OF BATTERIES

Motorhomes use two types of batteries, the first of which is the standard automotive SLI (**s**tart, **l**ights, **i**gnition) battery that you find in any vehicle. The SLI battery starts the engine and supplies power to the headlights, taillights, and other automotive functions and is almost always a liquid-electrolyte lead-acid battery as described in the previous section. SLI batteries are constructed to supply large amperages for a short time. Since discharge rates are directly related to plate surface area and the resultant diffusion rate of ions through the electrolyte, SLI batteries have many thin plates. This construction is the reason they cannot tolerate a deep discharge without severe damage.

The other battery type is one or more house batteries for powering your domestic appliances—all those electrical needs not associated with the normal operation of the vehicle on the road. A house battery should be a *deep-cycle battery*, which has heavier lead plates than an SLI battery, giving it greater capacity (albeit at a lesser rate of discharge) and the ability to withstand repeated heavy discharges such as those that occur during boondock camping. For this reason, our discussion will focus on deep-cycle batteries. These are what trailer RVs use. (For a complete discussion of all types of batteries, their properties, construction, and use, see our book *RV Electrical Systems*.)

Rule 1. Always use deep-cycle batteries for the house batteries of an RV's electrical system.

Deep-cycle batteries are further subdivided into traditional and sealed types as follows:

- **Wet-cell or flooded-electrolyte battery:** A lead-acid battery with a liquid electrolyte. This is like a typical starting battery but with heavier lead plates, and like a starting battery it has removable caps to permit inspection and servicing.

■ **Sealed immobilized-electrolyte battery:** A lead-acid battery that is sealed and cannot be serviced. It is often called a "maintenance-free" battery.

Sealed batteries are further subdivided into two types:

■ **Gel-cell battery:** A lead-acid battery in which the electrolyte is a gel or paste with the consistency of toothpaste or butter.

■ **Absorbed glass mat (AGM) battery:** A lead-acid battery in which the electrolyte is a liquid absorbed into sponge-like plate separators.

Most RVs come equipped with marine/RV 12-volt deep-cycle wet-cell batteries. While these are better suited for our purposes than a regular SLI battery, the better choices for a house battery are gel-cell, AGM, or golf-cart wet-cell batteries. All three types have proven their suitability. We installed two gel-cell batteries in our old trailer about ten years ago, when they were new on the scene. The batteries lasted seven years, which included a lot of boon-docking, and they were still going strong when we sold the trailer several years ago. (We're sorry now we didn't keep them. We had fine-tuned the charging voltage to just the right amount, and they gave us great service.)

However, each type of battery has its own advantages and disadvantages, which we'll cover next.

Wet-Cell Batteries

If you decide to use a wet-cell battery for your house battery, you can choose either a six-cell, 12-volt battery or a three-cell, 6-volt golf-cart battery.

A deep-cycle liquid-electrolyte 12-volt battery has several advantages:

■ relatively inexpensive

■ accepts high recharging voltages (see Chapter 9)

■ less likely to be affected by overcharging

■ good deep-cycle use with proper maintenance

■ lighter than other deep-cycle batteries

Its disadvantages are:

■ requires a battery box (so house batteries can be restrained in an upright position to avoid spills) and adequate ventilation

■ needs frequent maintenance (adding water and cleaning terminals)

■ has a higher rate of self-discharge than sealed batteries

■ is less rugged than golf-cart and sealed batteries

■ contains sulfuric acid, a dangerous corrosive that must be handled with extreme care

A golf-cart battery offers different advantages, which may better fit your needs:

- Has heavy lead plates that allow for a higher degree of discharge than SLI batteries or even regular deep-cycle batteries. (The plates are usually four times thicker than SLI battery plates and much heavier even than 12-volt deep-cycle wet-cell battery plates.) These batteries can occasionally be discharged to as much as 80% of their charge capacity, thus delivering power for a long period of time—an ideal characteristic for boondocking.

- Has a long life and is reasonably priced.

- Case is taller than other batteries, allowing for more battery capacity on the same "footprint" and more space under the plates to accommodate shedded material.

The disadvantages of a golf-cart battery are:

- It requires regular maintenance (and subsequent risk of dealing with sulfuric acid).

- The taller case may prove difficult to fit in a typical RV battery space, requiring a special battery box or compartment.

- Its ultra-thick plates do not provide the surface area necessary for high-amperage discharge loads.

- For the same reason, it requires longer recharging times than other batteries when deeply discharged.

Gel-Cell Batteries

Gel-cell batteries have large thin plates and either fiberglass or felt separators. The gelled electrolyte is pasted onto the plates and separators, which are then compressed tightly together during manufacturing. This technology results in a strong cell that will withstand vibration and shocks very well. Also because of the size and thinness of its plates, a gel-cell battery has a high rate of discharge and charge. Its charge absorption (acceptance) rate is likewise twice that of a deep-cycle wet-cell battery, thus allowing for a faster recharging time at a higher rate.

Gel-cell batteries are sealed batteries, meaning you can't get inside them, so they don't need maintenance. Although gassing is minimal with this design, overcharging can cause excessive oxygen and hydrogen to be produced. For this reason, they have valves to allow venting and thus are also called SVR (sealed valve regulated) or VRLA (valve regulated lead acid) batteries. When gassing does occur, it means the gel is drying out, and the battery's life is declining. To prevent gassing, limit charging voltages to 14.1 volts and below (see Chapter 9).

69

The advantages of a gel-cell battery are:

- minimal to no gassing and no risk of spills and corrosion
- no maintenance
- doesn't require ventilation
- good performance at low temperatures
- shock and vibration resistant
- excellent long life with many life cycles
- low self-discharge
- high discharge and charge-acceptance rates
- no sulfation

A gel-cell battery does have some disadvantages:

- high price tag
- heavier than wet-cell batteries
- requires accurate charge voltage regulation
- must not be overcharged

AGM Batteries

The AGM battery is the newest kid on the block. Its liquid electrolyte is contained in a sponge-like material of glass fibers, which is packed between the positive and negative plates. Like the gel-cell, this battery produces minimal gassing. The small amounts of oxygen and hydrogen produced are recombined within the battery, thus allowing automatic replenishing of the battery's water. This technology offers batteries that have both engine starting (SLI) capabilities and deep-cycle use.

An AGM battery has several advantages:

- minimal to no gassing and no risk of spills and corrosion
- no maintenance
- can be installed at any angle
- shock and vibration resistant
- excellent long life with many life cycles
- low self-discharge
- high discharge and charge-acceptance rates
- no sulfation

Its disadvantages are:

■ high price tag

■ heavier than deep-cycle wet-cell batteries

■ requires lower charging voltages than wet-cells when charging

■ does not tolerate extended overcharging

Many solar panel dealers recommend AGM batteries. Relative to other deep-cycle batteries, they seem to offer superior longevity and trouble-free service (this is particularly true of the Lifeline brand, www.lifelinebatteries.com). AGM batteries are usually charged at a slightly higher voltage than the gel-cells, which means it is easier to find charging equipment that will safely charge these batteries.

A word of caution: If you plan to buy a sealed, maintenance-free battery, be sure it is really a gel-cell or AGM battery. Some manufacturers produce wet-cell batteries containing extra electrolyte in partially sealed cases; such batteries should not be used as deep-cycle batteries.

Battery Sizes

Four basic 12-volt battery sizes serve most RVers' needs:

1. Group 24 batteries, with capacities ranging from 70 to 80 amp-hours (Ah). Singly, these are too small for practical RV use; they are best used in a bank of two or more.

2. Group 27 batteries, with capacities ranging from 80 to 105 Ah (the most common size).

3. 4D batteries, with capacities of 150 Ah and up (used in large Class A motorhomes).

4. 8D batteries, with capacities of 200 Ah and up (also used in large Class A's).

Table 8-1 gives battery specifications, including dimensions, for a selection of battery groups.

It is possible to buy 6-volt gel-cells and 6-volt AGMs with the same footprint or base size as 6-volt golf-cart wet-cells. (This footprint is, incidentally, the same size as a 12-volt Group 24 battery, the smallest 12-volt deep-cycle battery made for RV use.) The advantage to this is that more batteries will fit into a smaller space, and will still have the higher amp-hour rating of the golf-cart batteries.

Note that Table 8-1 includes two 6-volt golf-cart batteries with amp-hour ratings of 220 and 225 Ah, while the L16 6-volt battery has an impressive 370 Ah capacity. This battery has roughly the same footprint as a Group 27 12-volt battery but is 16 inches high, so it presents an installation problem.

Table 8-1. Battery Specifications						
Battery Part Number[1]	Amp-Hour Capacity Rating	Volts	Length (in.)	Width (in.)	Height (in.)	Weight (lbs.)
Lifeline AGM Batteries						
GPL-24T	80	12 V	11.13	6.77	9.25	56
GPL-27T	100	12 V	12.01	6.60	9.25	65
GPL-31T	105	12 V	12.90	6.75	9.27	69
GPL-4C	220	6 V	10.27	7.12	10.24	66
GPL-4DA	210	12 V	20.76	8.70	9.44	135
GPL-8DA	255	12 V	20.76	10.89	9.41	162
Exide Stowaway Wet-Cell Batteries						
BCI-24	80	12 V	10.18	6.81	9.43	—
BCI-27	105	12 V	12.00	6.81	9.50	—
BCI-31	115	12 V	13.00	6.75	9.87	—
BCI-4D	160	12 V	20.75	8.75	10.87	—
BCI-8D	200	12 V	20.75	11.00	10.87	—
Exide Golf-Cart Battery						
GC-110	220	6 V	10.38	7.13	10.88	62
West Marine SeaGel Gel-Cell Batteries						
GRP-24	73	12 V	10.87	6.75	9.88	54
GRP-27	86	12 V	12.75	6.75	9.88	64
GRP-31	97	12 V	12.94	6.75	9.38	72
GRP-4D	183	12 V	20.75	8.50	10.12	130
GRP-8D	225	12 V	20.75	11.00	10.00	161
GRP-6V	180	6 V	10.25	7.12	10.87	68
Trojan Golf-Cart Batteries						
T105	225	6 V	10.38	7.13	10.88	62
L16P	370	6 V	11.75	7.00	16.50	113
1. The group number is integrated into the part number; e.g., BCI-24 is a Group 24 battery. Note: Sealed batteries usually have lower amp-hour ratings than wet-cells.						

The 220 Ah golf-cart battery is about the same physical size as the Group 24 12-volt battery, except that it is taller by about 2 inches. Other battery sizes and groups may apply, but the above are the most common.

BATTERY CAPACITY: THE ELUSIVE AMP-HOUR

You've seen what deep-cycle batteries are available, and Table 8-1 assigns capacities to the various types, but how can the boondock RVer use these capacities to make informed choices? Before we can answer that question, we need to know what battery capacities mean in practice.

There Are Always Choices

We have always believed that a 12-volt battery system wired in parallel was better than a 6-volt system wired in series or series/parallel. (Series and parallel wiring are discussed later in this chapter.) The reason is that if a cell goes bad in one battery in the 12-volt system, you just disconnect the battery with the dead cell and use the other 12-volt battery until the dead battery can be replaced. If a cell in one of the batteries of a 6-volt two-battery bank goes bad, however, you lose the service of the whole bank, because the remaining 6-volt battery wouldn't have enough voltage to run the system.

Further, we have always believed that the most cost-effective choice of battery for this setup would be wet-cell batteries, and that the higher cost of sealed batteries wouldn't be justified by the benefits.

Recently, however, a friend pointed out something we had overlooked: golf-cart batteries have approximately the same footprint as the smaller Group 24 12-volt batteries. Thus, two 6-volt golf-cart batteries in series provide as much capacity as two larger Group 27 12-volt batteries in parallel while fitting into a smaller battery compartment (although you must account for the added height of about 2 inches). Making these 6-volt batteries the more expensive gel-cell or AGM type then makes sense, conferring the advantages of sealed batteries with their high amp-hour ratings in a smaller space.

The bottom line is that you have options when designing your own battery bank. Play around with different battery configurations (on paper) to determine what batteries will provide the best setup for your needs and space.

There are three main ways to determine battery capacity: amp-hour rating; cranking amps (cold cranking amps, CCA; or marine cranking amps, MCA); and reserve capacity rating. We focused on amp-hours in the above discussion of battery types because, for deep-cycle batteries, the amp-hour rating is far and away the most telling, but here we'll go over all three.

Amp-Hour Rating

As we learned earlier in the chapter, an ampere is the unit of measure for the flow rate of an electric current, and an amp-hour (Ah) is a measure of the total current that either has flowed or is capable of flowing from a battery or other power source for an hour. Put another way, the supply capacity of a battery is measured in amp-hours.

Say you have a water pump in your RV and you measure its current draw (using an ammeter) at 5 amps. If you run the water pump for 1 hour, you will have consumed 5 amp-hours of battery capacity:

$$5 \text{ amps} \times 1 \text{ hour} = 5 \text{ amp-hours}$$

If you run the pump for 15 minutes, you will have consumed 1.25 amp-hours:

$$5 \text{ amps} \times 0.25 \text{ hour} = 1.25 \text{ amp-hours}$$

Think of amperes as analogous to the instantaneous rate at which a vehicle is consuming gasoline, and think of amp-hours as the cumulative quantity of gasoline consumed over time. Most people know how many gallons of gasoline their fuel tank holds, and they have a fuel gauge to tell them when they need to fill up the tank. Similarly, we should know how much "gas" (in amp-hours) is stored in our batteries. There is, however, a difference between replenishing gasoline in a tank and amp-hours in a battery. Gasoline is replaced gallon for gallon, but due to battery inefficiencies, amp-hours must be replaced at a ratio of 1.2 amp-hours for every 1 amp-hour consumed.

Additionally there is likely to be a difference between the actual amp-hour capacity of a battery and the amp-hour rating assigned to it by the manufacturer. The actual capacity at any given time depends on the battery's state of charge as well as its temperature, its age, the size of the load imposed on it, and even the method used to measure its capacity. No wonder the average RVer can get very confused by the elusive amp-hour.

Load Size

While you can safely draw 1 amp from a 100 amp-hour battery every hour for 100 hours, you cannot draw 100 amps for 1 hour. The battery would be dead in about 20 minutes and would probably self-destruct. Heavy loads should never be applied to a battery continuously; as the load increases, the capacity decreases. For this very good reason, never apply a load greater than 25% of the amp-hour capacity of your battery. To do so greatly reduces the capacity rating.

Rule 2. Never apply a load greater than 25% of the battery capacity.

Temperature

Temperature often affects chemical reactions. In the case of batteries, as the air temperature drops, battery capacity decreases. For example, a battery that is at 100% of its rated capacity at 68°F would only retain about 85% of its capacity at 32°F, and only 70% at 0°F. This would mean that a 105 Ah battery would become a battery with a capacity of 89.25 Ah or 73.5 Ah respectively at the lower temperatures.

Age

As a wet-cell battery ages, it loses capacity because the unconverted sulfate forms clumps on the lead dioxide plates. When battery capacity has dropped to 75% to 80% of its capacity when new, it is time to replace it. You can tell a battery has reached this stage when, after a recharging and a 24-hour rest, the voltage is below 12.63 V or the specific gravity of even one cell is below 1.265 V (see Table 8-6 and pages 86–87).

Determining Amp-Hour Ratings

The most common and accurate way manufacturers determine the amp-hour rating of a battery is with a test called the amp-hour rate, or the 20-hour rate, which is usually performed at 80°F. A specific load of 5% of the estimated amp-hour capacity, usually from 4 to 11 amps, is applied to the fully charged battery until the battery voltage drops to 10.5 volts. If this takes 20 hours and the load is 5 amps, the battery will have a 100 amp-hour rated capacity:

20 hours × 5 amps = 100 amp-hours

The 20-hour rate was the standard for years, but now many manufacturers use test durations ranging from 5, 6, or 8 to 18, 25, or even 100 hours, with lower-amperage loads at the higher intervals, and at different temperatures.

When purchasing a battery, our best advice for determining amp-hour capacity is to look for specifications that are based on as long a time period as possible. These tests will probably be at a current-discharging rate similar to what you will normally be using to discharge your batteries.

It is possible to rate your own batteries when they are new, as follows:

1. Apply a load of a known value, say 5 amps (see Table 8-2).

2. Constantly check the battery voltage with a good-quality DC digital voltmeter (covered in Chapter 9).

3. Observe the time it takes for the voltage to drop to 10.5 volts.

4. Multiply that time by the amperage to get the amp-hour rating.

Table 8-2. Reserve Capacity at Various Amperage Rates

Load (amps)[1]	Group 24		Group 27	
	Time (hours)	Capacity (Ah)	Time (hours)	Capacity (Ah)
5	16.0	80	20.0	100
10	6.9	69	9.0	90
15	4.2	63	5.0	75
20	2.7	54	3.4	68
25	2.0	50	2.7	67.5

1. Differing loads affect the amp-hour rating of a battery. In normal use, loads vary both in amperage and the length of time they are applied, so these figures should be considered a guide rather than an accurate representation. Amp-hour ratings vary depending on the size of the battery, the manufacturer, and the method used to calculate the rating.

Cranking Amps

Two other battery ratings used by manufacturers are cold cranking amps (CCA) and marine cranking amps (MCA). These ratings refer to the amount of amperage available for starting an engine at either 0°F (CCA) or 60°F (MCA) and are strictly for rating engine starting batteries. (Some manufacturers use 32°F instead of 60°F in their MCA ratings.) These ratings have no relationship whatever to the deep-cycle batteries needed for house batteries in RVs. If a battery is rated in either CCA or MCA ratings, don't even consider buying it unless an amp-hour rating is also given (however, the chances are the battery will not be a true deep-cycle battery).

Reserve Capacity Rating

Another rating that has come into popular use by manufacturers is the reserve capacity rating, which gives the rating in reserve minutes (see Table 8-2). This method determines the number of minutes it takes for the battery voltage to reach 10.5 volts (a dead battery) with a 25 amp load applied. For example, a battery with a reserve capacity of 160 minutes would have a capacity of 66.67 amp-hours:

160 minutes × 25 amps = 4,000 amp-minutes ÷ 60 minutes = 66.67 amp-hours

This example shows how a high-amperage load can diminish the amp-hour capacity of a battery. The battery in this example would normally have an amp-hour capacity of 105 Ah, a common rating for a Group 27 wet-cell deep-cycle battery. Yet the equation above tells us the battery only has 66.67 amp-hours. An approximate way to convert reserve capacity to amp-hours is to multiply the reserve capacity by a factor of 0.65.

The reserve capacity rating is not suitable for rating an RV deep-cycle battery. Boondocking RVers seldom discharge their batteries at a steady 25 amp rate. Also, they certainly would not normally discharge them until the battery was completely dead at 10.5 volts. So the reserve capacity rating is not very useful for our purposes.

BUILDING A BATTERY BANK

By now it should be clear that amp-hour ratings are your best standard when selecting deep-cycle batteries. You can usually find these by searching the specification sheets from dealers and manufacturers. But one battery—regardless of type—will seldom be enough to satisfy all your boondocking power needs. More likely, you will have to wire together two or more batteries of a given type to form a bank. But how do you determine the number and size of batteries you will need? Here are some guidelines:

1. Determine your daily use. Estimate the total amp-hour consumption you think you might use in a typical night of battery use. You can use Table 8-3, and total your average night's usage of various appliances and lights.

2. To determine the battery storage capacity you'll need, multiply your amp-hour estimate from step 1 by 4. (We use 4 because, as explained in Chapter 9, we're considering the daily use estimate as 25% of the battery bank's amp-hour capacity.) This total will give you the approximate amp-hour battery capacity you may need.

3. Choose a type of battery. Based upon the information you've learned about the different types of batteries, choose one that will meet your needs: physical RV space, capacity, budget, etc. Do not combine batteries of different types or ratings in a bank.

4. Wire the batteries together to form the battery bank (see pages 81–82).

5. Monitor the electrical system to control amp-hour consumption (see Chapter 9 for more on monitoring batteries).

Determining Daily Battery Needs

To accurately determine the battery capacity you will need, you must first determine how much power you use on a daily basis. This exercise may seem a bit tedious, but is important to identify how much power you will be using, on average, when boondocking. It is also a good way to become familiar with the amount of power different items use so you can make informed choices about power consumption and battery charging. Your electrical needs won't be the same every night. For example, one night everyone may watch television for 1.5 hours, but the next night, the whole family wants to watch a 2-hour movie—except for

Table 8-3. Wattage and Amperage of 120 VAC and 12 VDC Appliances[1]			
Appliance[2]	AC Amps	DC Amps	Watts
Air conditioner, 7,100 Btu/h	10.00	—	1,200
Air conditioner, 13,500 Btu/h	14.16	—	1,700
Air conditioner, 14,800 Btu/h	16.00	—	1,920
Air conditioner, heat-strip	16.00	—	1,920
Blender	2.50	—	300
Coffeemaker	7.50	—	900
Computer, desktop	0.83	—	100
Computer printer	2.00	—	240
Converter/charger, 20 amp, at max. rating	3.50	—	420
Converter/charger, 30 amp, at max. rating	4.60	—	552
Converter/charger, 40 amp, at max. rating	5.50	—	660
Converter/charger, 75 amp, at max. rating	8.66	—	1,040
Cooler, evaporative, 12 V	—	6.0	72
Drill, $^3/_8$ in.	2.90	—	350
Dryer, hair	10.00	—	1,200
Equalizer/amplifier on stereo/cassette player	—	2.0	24
Fan, bathroom vent	—	2.0	24
Fan, range hood	—	2.0	24
Fan, roof vent, three-speed (depending on speed)	—	3.3	39
Fan, wall-mounted	—	1.2	14
Furnace, forced-air	—	8.0	96
Heater, electric, on 1,250 W setting	10.41	—	1,250
Heater, electric, 1,500 W	12.50	—	1,500
Iron, steam	10.83	—	1,300
Light, double fluorescent, 30 W	—	2.0	24
Light, single fluorescent, 8 W	—	0.7	8
Light, single fluorescent, 15 W	—	1.2	14
Light, double incandescent, type 1141 bulb	—	2.5	30
Light, single incandescent, type 1141 bulb	—	1.5	18
Light, double incandescent, type 1003 bulb	—	1.8	22
Light, single incandescent, type 1003 bulb	—	0.9	11
Microwave oven, small, 450 W rating	7.50	—	900
Microwave oven, large, 650 W rating	10.83	—	1,300
Radio, CB, receive-only mode	—	0.5	6
Refrigerator, 6 cu. ft., AC/gas, on AC	2.70	—	300
Refrigerator, 8 cu. ft., AC/gas, on AC	2.70	—	300
Refrigerator, portable, AC/DC	0.39	3.9	47
Refrigerator, three-way (Automatic Energy Selecting), on 12 V (figures shown are upper limits)	—	35.0	420

(continued)

Table 8-3. Wattage and Amperage of 120 VAC and 12 VDC Appliances[1] (continued)			
Appliance[2]	AC Amps	DC Amps	Watts
Refrigerator, 12 VDC, compressor-type	—	6.0	72
Saber saw	2.50	—	300
Sewing machine	1.25	—	150
Stereo/cassette player, automotive-type (figures shown are upper limits)	—	6.0	72
Toaster	7.50	—	900
TV, 5 in., B&W, AC/DC	0.15	1.5	18
TV, 9 in., color, AC/DC	0.45	4.5	54
TV, 13 in., color, AC/DC	0.58	5.8	70
TV, 21 in., color, AC	0.875	—	105
TV, 24 in., color, AC	1.08	—	130
TV satellite and receiver, AC	0.28	—	34
Vacuum cleaner, canister	2.91	—	350
Vacuum cleaner, handheld	2.00	—	240
VCR, AC	0.75	—	90
Videocassette player (VCP), AC/DC	0.15	1.5	18
Washer/dryer, RV type	16.00	—	1,920
Water pump	—	5.0	60

1. Beware of the amp-hogging equipment such as HDTVs, large-screen computer monitors, etc. Check the wattage before going boondocking with such items. We have a 25-inch TV that draws about 15 amps when run on an inverter. When boondocking, we use a 9-inch, 35-watt TV.
2. These ratings are approximate. Ratings vary between manufacturers and from product to product.

Dad, who wants to surf the Internet. Can the batteries handle both activities? Will you be able to recharge the batteries the next day?

To calculate your daily usage:

1. Identify the equipment and appliances you would generally use on a daily basis.

2. Find the amperage of each item using Table 8-3.

3. Estimate the amount of time you'll use each item, either in hours or percent of an hour. If you need a percent of an hour, you can either use Table 8-4 below for decimal equivalents, or convert hours and minutes to all minutes and divide by 60; for example:

$$47 \text{ minutes} \div 60 = 0.78 \text{ hour}$$

$$2 \text{ hours, } 33 \text{ minutes} = 153 \text{ minutes} \div 60 = 2.55 \text{ hours}$$

4. Multiply amps by time to get amp-hours.

Table 8-4. Time/Decimal Equivalents	
Time (min.)	Decimal Equivalents of an Hour
1	0.0167
5	0.0834
10	0.167
15	0.250
20	0.334
30	0.500
40	0.667
50	0.833
60	1.000

Table 8-5. Daily Usage Example	
Appliance	Usage (Ah)
Two 12 V lights @ 1.5 amps each for 4 hours	12.00
Color TV @ 54 watts (120 VAC) for 3 hours	13.50
Satellite receiver @ 34 watts (120 VAC) for 3 hours	8.50
Water pump @ 5 amps for 10 minutes	0.83
Refrigerator @ 0.2 amp on propane for 15 hours	3.00
Total	37.83

Let's illustrate the above with an example of items you might use over the course of an average day:

- 12-volt lights; the two most popular 12-volt lightbulbs are the #1003 at 1 amp and the #1141 at 1.5 amps (see Table 8-3)

- TV and satellite dish receiver, both running on 12 VDC off an inverter

- water pump

- phantom load, such as the refrigerator—even on propane, the refrigerator draws some amperage and accumulates some amp-hours (we'll cover phantom loads in detail shortly)

Given these appliances, a corresponding daily usage is shown in Table 8-5. (Converting watts to amp-hours is explained in the following section.)

Eliminating the color TV and satellite receiver would reduce the daily consumption to 15.83 amp-hours, thus allowing for a much smaller battery bank capacity.

Calculating Amp-Hours in a DC/AC System

One of the problems when calculating amp-hours in a system that supplies both DC and AC loads is that you are mixing apples and

Large TVs in New RVs

The RV industry currently seems to believe that all RV buyers want large TVs—19-, 21-, or 24-inch or even larger models—in their new units. These sets may be nice to look at, but they exact a huge toll in battery consumption. Larger sizes can consume up to 175 watts. When on inverter power, this amounts to a draw of up to 14.6 amps (175 watts ÷ 12 volts) on your battery bank; 3 hours' use would equate to 43.75 amp-hours, a hefty discharge for only a few hours of television viewing. If you have one of these behemoths, we suggest using it only when you have campground power and getting a small 9-inch AC/DC set for boondocking. That is what we have used for over twenty years, and we've been happy with it. The newer ones even have built-in DVD players.

oranges. You must convert AC amps to DC amps to calculate amp-hours. Here is an easy conversion method:

1. Convert all 120-volt AC and 12-volt DC appliances and equipment into watts (watts = amps × volts). Watts are watts, whether AC or DC.

2. Multiply each item by the hours used to get the number of watt-hours.

3. Divide the total watt-hours by 12 volts to get amp-hours.

As an example, let's look at the color TV and satellite receiver from Table 8-5. The color TV draws 0.45 amp at 120 volts AC, which is 54 watts, and the satellite receiver draws 0.28 amp at 120 VAC, which is 34 watts. For 3 hours of usage:

TV: 54 watts × 3 hours = 162 watt-hours

Receiver: 34 watts × 3 hours = 102 watt-hours

Total watt-hours: 162 watt-hours + 102 watt-hours = 264 watt-hours

Total amp-hours: 264 watt-hours ÷ 12 volts = 22 amp-hours

Ohm's Law

Ohm's Law explains the mathematical relationship between current (amps), voltage (volts), and resistance (ohms). It is expressed as:

$$I \text{ (current)} = V \text{ (voltage)} \div R \text{ (resistance)}$$

There are several variations of this formula:

$$I = V \div R$$
$$V = R \times I$$
$$R = V \div I$$

Now let's add a fourth element, *power*, or the rate at which work is done, measured in watts. Just like volts, amps, and ohms, watts can be calculated easily:

$$P = V \times I$$
$$V = P \div I$$
$$I = P \div V$$

If you know any two components, you can calculate the third. For example, let's say you want to know how many amps (I) a 120-volt (V), 1,000-watt (W) microwave will draw. The equation would look this:

$$I = 1,000 \text{ watts} \div 120 \text{ volts} = 8.3 \text{ amps}$$

While the formulas are simple, some of us may find it easier to remember visuals. The triangle gives a graphical perspective of the equations. If you place your finger over any one of the components, you'll see how to calculate that value.

Ohm's Law triangle.

Determining Storage Capacity

Once you've estimated your daily amp-hour usage, you can estimate the size of the battery bank you'll need. Because we advocate not discharging batteries by more than 25% of their amp-hour capacity (see Chapter 9), we'll use 4 as our multiplier. The total will be a good estimate of the amount of storage capacity you'll need. To supply the 37.83 amp-hours in Table 8-5, you'd need a battery bank capacity of at least 150 Ah, which you could get from two Group 24 12-volt batteries wired in parallel or (more comfortably) from two 6-volt batteries wired in series. If you wanted to supply that same demand for two or three days, you'd either need a very large battery bank or you'd need to do some recharging as discussed in Chapters 10 through 12.

Wiring Batteries in Series and Parallel

All batteries are classed by their voltage, with 12-volt batteries being the standard because that is the voltage used in most RVs. When 6-volt batteries are used, they are wired together in series to make a bank of 12 volts.

To wire batteries in series, connect the positive terminal of one battery to the negative terminal of the other. When wired this way, voltage is additive and capacity remains the same. Two 6-volt, 220 amp-hour batteries wired in series will yield 12 volts and a 220 amp-hour capacity.

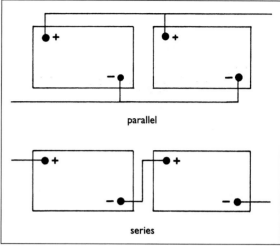

Wiring batteries in series and parallel.

A word of caution: If you have a 12-volt system in your RV, **never** wire two 12-volt batteries in series. You'd end up with a 24-volt battery bank, which would damage your 12-volt appliances and equipment.

When wiring batteries in parallel, connect positive terminals to positive terminals and negative terminals to negative terminals. Voltage remains the same, but capacity (amp-hours) is additive. For example, if you wire two Group 24 12-volt batteries, each with a 73 amp-hour capacity, in parallel, you'll have a 12-volt battery bank with a capacity of 146 amp-hours.

Understanding these two wiring options gives you flexibility. If you want to use 6-volt batteries for your battery bank, you can join multiple 6-volt batteries to get the storage capacity you need. First wire the batteries in pairs in series to make 12 volts, and then wire each pair in parallel to double the amp-hour capacity.

For example, say you have four 6-volt batteries, and each battery has a capacity of 220 Ah. Wiring each pair in series yields 12 volts, with a 220 Ah capacity. Wiring both pairs in parallel yields a bank of 12 volts with a 440 Ah capacity. Eight similarly wired batteries would yield a 12-volt bank of 880 Ah. Multiple banks of 12-volt batteries in series and parallel are used for the 24-volt house systems common to many large bus conversions.

6-Volt vs. 12-Volt Batteries

There is a bit of controversy over whether 6-volt or 12-volt batteries are better in a battery bank. Two of the arguments for using 6-volt batteries are (1) there are fewer cables involved in series wiring, so there are fewer connections to corrode; and (2) in 12-volt parallel wiring, one of the batteries in a two-battery bank will receive most of the load and most of the charge, and therefore will fail faster than the other.

The first argument has some validity as there are fewer cables in series wiring, so there is less corrosion. The second argument is not necessarily true, if you wire the bank as shown above. If a battery goes bad in a 12-volt bank, you can just disconnect it and use the remaining one. You'll still be getting 12 volts. With a 6-volt bank, however, one bad battery means the loss of the whole two-battery bank.

The number of batteries you can have often depends on the available space in your RV. Our RV was designed to hold two Group 24 batteries. When we decided we wanted to use two Group 27 gel-cell batteries, we had to lengthen the battery compartment to hold them. And if you decide you want to use golf-cart batteries, you'll have to accommodate their height.

PHANTOM LOADS

One issue that can be a problem when boondocking is that of phantom loads, also called parasitic loads, idling current, or standby current. Phantom loads are caused by any device that consumes amperage whether it is on or off.

For example, our refrigerator is the typical AC/propane type used in most RVs. What is not commonly known is that these refrigerators use 12-volt DC power whether the main power source is 120-volt AC or propane. Altogether, when our refrigerator is operating on propane it draws 0.9 amp.

Over a 24-hour period, this level of consumption has the potential for depleting the batteries by a whopping 21.6 amp-hours. We say "potential" because the amperage draw will fluctuate as the propane is turned on and off, and we do not use the high-humidity setting. However, the point is still valid—small amperage draws can add up and may catch you unawares. Here are the numbers:

- storage switch in the On position draws 0.2 amp

- automatic ignition system (for lighting the propane) draws 0.5 amp

- high-humidity setting draws 0.2 amp

Other examples of appliances and equipment that have phantom loads are listed below. You can see that the list includes both 12-volt DC and 120-volt AC items.

- TVs with circuits that maintain channel-memory settings and provide for fast start-ups

- satellite receivers with live circuits that maintain programming information

- microwave ovens with timers and clocks

- clocks, stereos, and radios

- pilot lights

- switches with LEDs that indicate a device is on

- VCRs and VCPs

- RV refrigerators

- propane and carbon monoxide detectors

- security systems
- automatic-ignition propane water heaters

An RV can have several or all of these items installed, and the phantom-load effect is cumulative. Even milliamps of current draw can be significant. A draw of 500 milliamps equals 0.5 amp, and over 24 hours, would amount to a 12 amp-hour depletion. Several low-milliamp devices added together could cause quite a drain on your batteries. Car stereos are often used in RVs as the entertainment center to provide AM/FM radio and either cassette or CD music. These units all have phantom loads due to the push-button station selection memory and built-in clocks.

If you are using a large inverter to power your AC appliances, eliminating phantom loads will reduce the load drawn by the inverter. Why draw 20 amps when all you need is 10 or 15 amps for the job? Remember that for every amp of 120-volt AC current used, you are drawing approximately 10 amps at 12 volts from your batteries (1 AC amp = 10 DC amps).

It was customary some years ago for some RV manufacturers, particularly those who made motorhomes, to install an inexpensive 13-inch AC-only color TV. They then supplied a small, cheap 100-watt inverter to power it. This practice provided a constant phantom load since the inverter was always on and the TV, even though it may have been turned off, was still drawing a small amount of current.

If you have this type of installation on your rig, install a switch on the DC circuit to the inverter. Use an in-line switch and install it on the inverter cord. When the TV is not being used, you can turn it off at the switch.

More generally, you can eliminate phantom loads by installing in-line switches on all of your devices and appliances and turning them off when you're not using the items. For example, we have a power strip with a switch on it that we use to power the TV and the satellite receiver. When we run anything else on the inverter, we first turn off the strip and then the refrigerator so that we can be sure these phantom loads are removed from the inverter before we turn on the other appliances. Jan says Bill is "switch happy" because he puts switches on everything, but he believes it is the best insurance against phantom loads. This applies to both 12-volt DC and 120-volt AC devices, with the latter becoming ever more prominent in RVs.

Another solution is even simpler. Just switch off or unplug any appliance not being used so it will not operate inadvertently when on either generator or inverter power.

WET-CELL BATTERY SAFETY

Most of us are rather cavalier in the handling of our automotive and RV wet-cell batteries. After all, they're part of our everyday RV life. They usually give us good service and the life expectancy we think they should, so it's rather natural for us to take them for granted. And when a battery fails to start the engine and needs to be recharged, we matter of factly connect it to someone else's battery for a jump start. We rarely even consider the possible danger.

Lurking in a wet-cell battery, however, are two hazardous and potentially dangerous ingredients: sulfuric acid and hydrogen gas. Sulfuric acid is corrosive and can severely burn skin and eyes on contact. If you get it on your clothes, it will eat away at the cloth.

Bill has had some personal experience with the effects of sulfuric acid. When still in high school, he got a good-paying summer job working at a battery factory. After two weeks, and in spite of wearing heavy gloves and a rubber apron, he had acid sores on his hands from handling the batteries. One day he was walking down an aisle carrying a battery and the entire front of his fairly new jeans disintegrated from their brief exposure to sulfuric acid. That's when he decided to quit—and the boss had a good laugh.

Hydrogen gas can be even more deadly because it is explosive. Please take this gas seriously. Batteries have been known to explode because of hydrogen gas at the terminals, usually during charging and with poor ventilation, and an exploded battery is not a pretty sight.

We don't mean to scare you into avoiding batteries altogether, but you should be aware of the hazards and use caution when handling batteries.

Safety Practices

Here is a basic list of safety practices for working around wet-cell lead-acid batteries. It is not exhaustive. You should also check any manufacturer's instructions or documentation that came with your battery.

- Do not smoke, because of the possible presence of hydrogen gas and the risk of an explosion.

- Wear goggles, or even better, a full-face shield to protect your eyes and face from acid. Sulfuric acid in your eyes can cause blindness.

- Always wear heavy-duty rubber gloves. The best gloves are ones like those worn by commercial fishermen.

- Wear a rubber or plastic apron to protect your clothes and body from acid spills.

- Do not charge your batteries with the vent caps off. If the caps are off when the full gassing stage is reached, the acid can bubble up and splatter over you and maybe even reach your face and eyes.

- Keep a jar of baking soda nearby. Pour it on any spills or on your hands if they come in contact with acid.

- Have a bucket of clean water handy to wash away acid in case of major spills and accidents. If an item becomes contaminated with acid, plunge it into the water. Immerse acid-contaminated clothing in the bucket to stop possible damage. But do not use this water to flush your eyes if you get acid in them. If anything has been rinsed off in the bucket, the water will contain acid.

■ Keep a large bottle of water close by in case acid gets into your eyes. Pour water into your eyes to help stop further damage, then quickly get to a faucet. Flush your eyes with running water for 15 minutes. Get immediate medical attention.

WET-CELL BATTERY MAINTENANCE

Battery maintenance varies with the type of battery you have. Sealed batteries (gel-cell and AGM batteries) usually require only an occasional cleaning of the top of the batteries. Wet-cell batteries, however, need a consistent maintenance program to keep them operating to their full capacity. Basic maintenance tasks are outlined below.

You'll need the following tools and supplies in addition to the safety items mentioned above:

■ hydrometer

■ wire brush

■ distilled water

■ lubricating spray (e.g., WD-40)

■ dielectric grease

■ pump pliers

■ two $1/2$-inch, open-end wrenches

■ baking soda

■ water

■ paper towels

■ mirror

■ flashlight

Inspect and Clean the Battery Case

Before doing anything, check the battery case itself for cracks, corrosion, or other obvious signs of damage. Look for any fluid on the case, which may indicate leaks in the battery case. Inspect connections, looking for broken or frayed cables or damaged parts.

Always clean the top of the battery when you do maintenance work. Wet or greasy dirt on the top can create pathways for current to leak between the posts, which will discharge the battery. Regular cleaning is especially important for batteries mounted on the tongue of a conventional trailer, where they have less protection from dirt, and for those on diesel-fueled vehicles as the soot produced from diesel fuel is a particularly bad contaminant for the electrolyte.

1. Be sure the cell caps are tightened before you begin cleaning. Any dirt or cleaning solution that gets into the electrolyte will shorten the life of the battery.

2. Remove dirt from around the cell caps using a damp paper towel or wire brush. If the dirt is greasy, use a dry paper towel.

3. Clean the case with a solution of baking soda and water; use 1 teaspoon of baking soda in 4 ounces of water. This solution will dissolve the crud that can build up on the terminals of the batteries. Pour it on the terminals and wipe up with paper towels. We usually use paper cups with one side pinched together to form a pouring spout for the soda solution.

4. Clean the terminals and inside the cable clamps with a wire brush. You can use the baking soda solution here as well, if needed.

5. Coat the terminals with Vaseline, or even better, dielectric grease (you can buy this at any automotive parts store). Dielectric grease will ensure all connections to the terminal have a good solid electrical contact with no resistance. It will also prevent the battery cables from corroding. (Note: Corrosion only occurs on wet-cell battery terminals and is caused by the hydrogen and oxygen gases that escape through the vent caps during charging. Corrosion can eat away battery cable connections until only the terminals are left.)

Check the Specific Gravity

Specific gravity is the ratio of the density of a substance to the density of water. The electrolyte in a lead-acid battery is a solution of sulfuric acid and water. The sulfuric acid is more dense than water so as the battery discharges, the acid becomes less dense. Thus the specific gravity of the electrolyte is a measure of the battery's state of charge. Specific gravity is measured with a battery hydrometer calibrated for the range of electrolyte densities normally found in a battery, 1.000 to 1.3000. (Note: There are different kinds of hydrometers; make sure you get one for use with batteries.)

When an electrolyte sample is drawn into the hydrometer, a float indicates the specific gravity. However, the indicated reading must be corrected to what it would be at a standard temperature, often 77°F, but use whatever temperature your hydrometer calls for.

As we all know, battery compartments in an RV are usually cramped. You may have to remove the battery for this test if there isn't enough room above the battery to maneuver the hydrometer. Remember, wear heavy-duty rubber gloves to protect your hands.

1. Do not add water first.

2. Insert the hydrometer into a cell. Fill and drain the tube two to four times before taking a sample to read.

3. For the sample draw, be sure to fill the tube completely so the float is floating.

4. Record the reading and return the electrolyte to the cell.

5. Repeat these steps for each cell.

6. Replace the cell caps and wipe off any spilled electrolyte.

Calculate the State of Charge

To calculate the state of charge, you need to convert your specific gravity readings to volts:

1. Compare the readings of the cells. If the reading of any individual cell varies by more than 50 points from the other cells, the cell may be bad; you should replace the battery.

2. Otherwise average the readings and add 0.84 (a constant) to this number.

3. Multiply this figure by the number of cells in the battery.

4. The resulting voltage is the state of charge.

Here is an example using a 12-volt wet-cell battery with six cells. If the average specific gravity equals 1.265:

$$1.265 \text{ (specific gravity)} + 0.84 \text{ (constant)} = 2.105$$
$$2.105 \times 6 \text{ (number of cells)} = 12.63 \text{ V (state of charge)}$$

You can also use a table, such as Table 8-6 on page 88.

Check the Electrolyte Level

It is important to check the level of the electrolyte acid at least once a month, and more often during hot weather. Never allow the electrolyte level to fall below the top of the plates in the cells. This will cause the plates to overheat and buckle, ruining the battery.

1. Charge the batteries before adding water to the cells. Electrolyte expands during the charging process. Filling the cells first can result in overfilling, and excess electrolyte will bubble out during charging. The only exception to this is if the electrolyte is below the top of the plates. If you encounter this, add just enough water to cover the plates and then charge the battery.

2. After charging, allow the battery to rest for several hours so the charge can equalize throughout the battery.

Table 8-6. Battery Capacity by Specific Gravity and Voltage				
Remaining Capacity (%)	% of Discharge	Specific Gravity @ 77°F	Volts per Cell	12-Volt Nominal Battery Voltage
100	0	1.265	2.106	12.63[1]
90	10	1.251	2.091	12.54
80	20	1.236	2.076	12.45
70	30	1.221	2.061	12.36
60	40	1.206	2.046	12.27
50	50	1.191	2.031	12.18
40	60	1.176	2.016	12.09
30	70	1.161	2.001	12.00
20	80	1.146	1.986	11.91
0	100	1.131	1.971	11.82

1. Other tables that give the voltage of fully charged batteries as 12.7 or 12.8 volts were compiled using temperatures other than 77°F.

3. Before adding water to the cells, turn off all loads and the battery charger to prevent acid from bubbling up.

4. Remove each cap separately and check the electrolyte level. Wear goggles or a face shield when doing this to protect your eyes. Otherwise, we recommend using a mirror and flashlight. Direct the flashlight beam into the mirror to bounce the light into the cell. You'll see the inside of the cell in the mirror without placing your face over the cell.

5. If the level is low, add ONLY distilled water. (Spring water or any other non-distilled water has mineral deposits that will ruin your battery.) **Do not** overfill or you will not leave enough space under the cell cap for gassing.

6. Replace cell caps and wipe off any spilled liquid.

The above may sound like a lot of work—initially. However, after you've done it a few times, it really isn't that bad. The advantage is, of course, a long life of good service from your wet-cell batteries.

CHAPTER 9

Monitoring and Charging Your Batteries

So far we've looked at the basics of batteries, as well as how to calculate daily power consumption and build a battery bank. In this chapter we'll cover how to monitor the state of charge in your batteries, which will tell you when you need to charge them, as well as battery-charging methods.

MONITORING YOUR BATTERIES

It is never a good idea to go into the wilderness without a system in place that allows you to easily and regularly monitor your batteries' state of charge. This not only helps

(RVIA)

you manage your resources properly while boondocking, so you get the most comfort and pleasure out of the experience, but also protects the life span of your batteries. Improper discharging and charging will guarantee that you'll be buying new batteries frequently. And unfortunately, the typical battery condition meter installed in an RV's monitor panel is not accurate enough, so you'll probably need to get some other equipment. The most common monitoring meters used for measuring current and voltage are ammeters and voltmeters.

Ammeters

Ammeters measure the flow of amps within an electrical system. They can be very useful for determining how big an amp load the system is drawing from your batteries at any one time and for monitoring your battery-charging system. There are two types of ammeters used in RVs, series and shunt.

Series Ammeters

A series ammeter is inserted into the positive wire between the battery and the fuse panel. Because it is directly in the circuit, the full current flows through the ammeter, allowing it to measure both load currents from the battery and charging currents from the various charging devices to the battery.

To monitor battery usage with this device, take meter readings every hour over the course of the evening, then add them up at the end of the night. This figure will give you an approximate amp-hour consumption. If you used about 6 amps per hour for 6 hours, you would have depleted your batteries by roughly 36 amp-hours.

Although the series ammeter is a bit outdated today, it is still probably the simplest way to monitor battery usage. We used a series ammeter for years on our older RVs. These meters have several advantages: they are available at most auto parts stores, are inexpensive, and are simple to wire. And they work well if you use a little common sense.

The series ammeter does have a few disadvantages. Because it is installed in the circuit between the battery and the fuse panel, it requires a very heavy wire to handle the current flowing through it. In most cases, you'll need 4 AWG or larger wire. This location usually means the meter is in an inconvenient place for frequent monitoring, and routing the heavy wire to a more convenient location may be both expensive and impractical.

Another disadvantage relates to its scale. The most common series ammeter has a scale ranging from −60 amps to 0 to +60 (−60–0–+60) amps (the negative readings are discharges and the positives are charging). With this scale range, the numerical markings are in 5 or 10 amp increments, making it too large for accurate battery readings. Such a meter can only show approximate readings.

You can get ammeters with smaller scales, although they may be harder to find. In our first fulltiming trailer we mounted a −20–0–+20 meter on the front of the dinette seat, which was where the fuse panel was installed. This meter measured 1 amp increments but only went up to 20 amps, which is small by today's standards.

Shunt Ammeters

A shunt ammeter is really a sensitive voltmeter that measures amps instead of volts. It has two components. The shunt is a conductor of known resistance that is inserted directly into the circuit through which the full current flows. The meter is connected to the shunt by a lightweight wire. A small portion of the current is diverted from the circuit to flow through the meter.

As current flows through the shunt ammeter, it causes voltage drop (see Chapter 10).

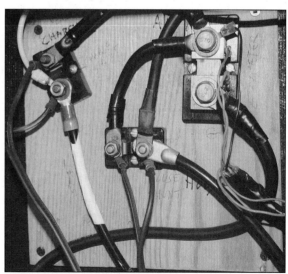

My shunt ammeter has a knob that lets you choose between volts and two ammeters, allowing you to monitor both charging and discharging amperages.

The ammeter determines the amperage by measuring this voltage drop. For example, if a shunt has 0.5 ohm of resistance and the measured voltage drop is 1 volt, the current flow (from Ohm's Law—see Chapter 8) is 2 amperes.

The primary advantage of a shunt ammeter is that you can locate the meter wherever it is convenient for you to view. Because only a small portion of the current flows to the meter, you can use lightweight 16 to 20 AWG wire for this connection, making it easy to route and inexpensive.

Shunt ammeters can be analog or digital. The digital models provide a higher level of accuracy, with readings to either a tenth or a hundredth of an amp, making them more useful than analog meters. Needless to say, however, the digital models are more expensive.

Another disadvantage of most digital meters is that they do not identify the readings as either positive or negative. A reading is usually the difference between the negative and positive readings, and it must be interpreted correctly.

Our shunt board for different instruments measuring amperage, voltage, and amp-hours. A setup like this is not normally needed on an RV, but we use it for the tests we run.

Here are a few examples:

- Your solar panel is delivering a charge of 6 amps, and you have a light on and several other phantom loads creating a discharge of 2.5 amps. The meter will show a net reading of 3.5 amps, and without a plus/minus sign you must interpret which way the current is flowing. (A charging current would register as a positive value if your meter gave plus/minus signs.)

- You have a discharge of 5 amps and a charge of 2 amps. The meter will show 3 amps, which would be a negative figure.

You must always figure out from what you know or can infer from the reading whether it is a positive or negative value.

One solution to this problem is to have two ammeters, one in the positive wire and another in the negative one. This way you can measure both discharging and charging currents at the same time. However, this also increases the expense.

Voltage Meters

Voltmeters measure the voltage present in the system, and it would seem logical that you could use this to ascertain a battery or battery bank's state of charge. A fully charged battery at 77°F should measure 12.63 volts across the two battery terminals. A completely discharged battery has a voltage of 11.82 volts. A battery that has been discharged to 50% of its capacity will, in theory, show a voltage of 12.18. (As mentioned earlier, most battery manufacturers consider 10.5 volts the reading at which a battery is really dead, but any battery with a voltage reading of 11.8 or lower isn't going to run much of anything.)

In practice, any load (lights, etc.) applied to the battery will cause a temporary voltage drop proportional to the size of the load, and the reading under this load will be less than the battery's resting voltage. By the same token, if the battery bank is being charged, the meter will show a surface charge voltage caused by the charging process, not the true resting-state charge, and the result is a falsely high reading. A fully charged battery will give a highly accurate voltage reading only when the battery has rested for 24 hours—without load or charge—to allow the voltage to equalize between the cells.

A 24-hour rest is impractical in most cases, of course, so we have found by experimentation that an approximate state of battery charge can be measured after resting the battery bank (by turning off all loads and charging sources) for about 5 minutes.

This is enough time to allow the voltage to partially equalize across the cells, thus giving a somewhat truer reading. Longer resting periods will give more accurate readings, at least up to 3 hours. After that you may have reached the point of diminishing returns.

Checking battery voltage with a panel-mounted analog voltmeter or an analog multimeter won't give you what you need to know, because there aren't enough incremental markings for accuracy. Most analog (needle-type) voltmeters have a possible error greater than the

0.81-volt difference between a fully charged battery and a fully discharged one. A digital meter that reads to only one decimal place isn't accurate enough either.

The so-called battery condition meters installed in most RV monitoring panels are therefore worthless. There are, however, expensive analog battery condition meters that have an expanded scale between 10 and 15 volts. These meters, which usually read as a percentage of charge, will help you interpret the voltage more accurately than a regular voltage meter, but they still fail to give a completely reliable picture.

Panel-mounted voltmeters and multi-meters with digital readings to at least two decimal points can give very accurate readings and will have 81 increments between the fully charged and fully discharged states. The resultant readings must be interpreted properly, however.

Such readings can be used to monitor state of charge if taken hourly as current is drawn from the batteries. Allow the batteries to rest (no load, no charge)

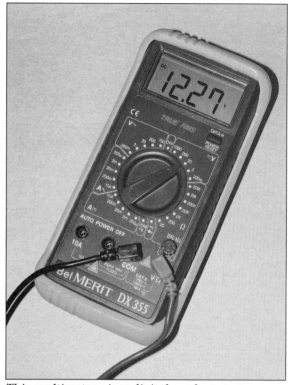

This multimeter gives digital readouts to two decimal points.

at least 5 minutes before each reading is made. Soon you will have a good idea of the differences between readings made with and without loads, and by applying this knowledge you can get a good estimate of your battery bank's state of charge. Most authorities believe batteries should never be discharged to voltages below 12.1 volts if you want long battery life.

Note: It will be easier to use a multimeter if you install a special 12-volt outlet where you'll be using the unit. Then make up special wire leads with a 12-volt plug on one end and meter jacks on the other. We used this method for years before fancier meters came along. And once you have a 12-volt DC source—DO NOT USE A CIGARETTE LIGHTER PLUG—use any plug as long as it is not a standard household plug. Check marine supply catalogs and stores; they offer a variety of 12-volt plugs.

Voltmeters do have other uses. For example, they will tell you if your batteries are being charged (by virtue of the high surface voltage reading you will see), and the voltage reading mode of a multimeter is useful for troubleshooting electrical problems.

Amp-Hour Meters

The best way to monitor your RV batteries' state of charge is with an amp-hour meter. With this meter, you can know for sure how many amp-hours you've consumed, when it is time to recharge the batteries again, and when the batteries are completely recharged. It also provides amp readings and other useful features.

Amp-hour meters are usually adjusted to read 000, or slightly higher, when the battery is fully charged. As amp-hours are removed from the battery, a counter shows a negative number, indicating the cumulative amp-hours consumed. So if you have a 105 Ah battery, and the meter shows 26 Ah, you've used 25% of the battery's capacity. If the meter shows 52 Ah, you've discharged 50% of the battery and it is definitely time to recharge. (If at all possible, never discharge batteries more than 50%.) As you recharge the battery, the meter will add back amp-hours; when the meter again reads zero, the battery has been recharged to 100% of capacity. (These meters take into account the charging inefficiency of the 1 to 1.2 Ah charging factor.)

Rule 3: Always monitor battery consumption; if possible, use an amp-hour meter.

Today there are amp-hour meters that incorporate other monitoring features: ammeters, voltmeters, time left to total discharge, and a light signal indicating when the batteries are fully recharged. Many of these fancier meters are incorporated into the monitoring panels of inverters and chargers, so that you can get all functions into one panel. These panels also have the capability of turning the inverter or charging device on and off as needed.

The control panel of the Xantrex Battery Monitor, which measures amp-hours. (Xantrex)

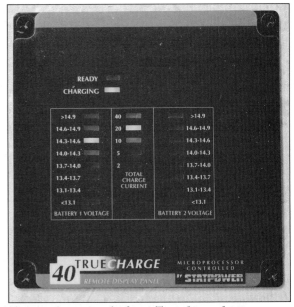

The readout panel of our Truecharge battery charger.

If you have problems finding suitable meters from RV stores, Camping World (www.campingworld.com), or RV supply houses, try marine catalogs or look online. West Marine is a good source (www.westmarine.com); it has a good selection of meters—both analog and digital—as well as plugs and sockets.

CHARGING YOUR BATTERIES

As we learned in Chapter 8, a chemical reaction takes place within a battery as electrical energy is removed from it. To recharge the battery, we pass an electrical current through it in order to reverse the reaction and restore the battery's original composition.

> ### Our Monitoring System
>
> Over the years, we have developed a sophisticated monitoring system incorporating several different meters.
>
> - an amp-hour meter to record the amp-hours being consumed or charged
> - ammeters to read the charging amps of each of our four different charging devices
> - an ammeter located so as to read the total amps being used at any time
> - a voltmeter to monitor the AC voltage output of the inverter or generator
>
> You may not want and probably don't need a system as complicated as ours, especially since most of this data is available from a good-quality amp-hour meter.

One big misconception concerning battery charging is that amperage charges a battery. Not so—voltage charges a battery. This confusion is understandable since battery chargers are rated by their amperage (such as a 50 amp charger or a 100 amp alternator). Amperage in this case is a measure of the rate of current flow from the charging source to the battery and thus a measure of the speed of recharging, but it is not the *cause* of recharging. You could hook a 50 amp charger to a discharged battery and throw the switch, but unless the charger has a higher voltage potential than the discharged battery, there will be no charging current at all, much less 50 amps' worth.

Rule 4. Voltage recharges a battery, not amperage.

A battery that has a voltage lower than its fully charged level of 12.63 volts can be recharged by applying a charging source at a higher voltage. Within reason, the higher the voltage applied, the greater the charge-current amperage and the faster the recharge (there are limitations to this, as we will see). In other words, when a source of higher voltage is connected to a battery of lower voltage, a current will flow between the source and the battery until the battery's voltage rises to equal the source voltage. In practice the charging voltage should be at least 1 volt higher than the battery's fully charged voltage level of 12.63. This establishes a minimum charging voltage of 13.63.

But there is also a maximum acceptable charging voltage, and it varies according to the type of battery. Charging voltages higher than 14.5 are bad for wet-cell batteries because the liquid electrolyte boils vigorously, causing severe gassing and creating heat. If allowed to continue, this reduces the electrolyte volume and results in severe overcharging, both of which will damage the battery. Yet wet-cell batteries will not fully charge unless the charging voltage

Table 9-1. Wet-Cell Voltage Variations[1] Due to Temperature		
Temperature (°F)	Voltage at Gassing	Float Voltage (see later in chapter)
37	14.49	13.59
57	14.44	13.59
77	14.40	13.54
97	14.36	13.46
117	14.31	13.41

1. Although the incremental voltage variations may not seem very important, they can greatly affect the charging rate.

Table 9-2. Voltages Needed to Recharge Various Battery Types	
Battery Type	Voltage
Wet-cell	14.4
AGM	14.2–14.3
Gel-cell	14.0–14.1

is maintained at the gassing level of 14.3 to 14.5 volts. Many charging devices do not charge to these high levels of voltage.

Temperature affects both voltage and gassing. As the temperature increases, the voltage at which gassing occurs decreases. Many high-quality charging devices have temperature sensors that vary the voltage to match the ambient temperature. Putting all this together, we find that charging a wet-cell battery to its fullest requires the voltage to reach 14.4 volts, the gas point, at 77°F. Table 9-1 shows how temperature changes affect the gassing voltage.

Gel-cell batteries, however, require a lower charging voltage level because gassing must be minimized in these sealed batteries. Thus, they are only charged to a level of 14.0 to 14.1 volts, depending on the battery manufacturer's specifications. Higher voltage will cause over-charging, drying out the paste or gel electrolyte. Several years ago when we had two gel-cell batteries we adjusted the charger voltage to a set point of 14.1 volts, and the batteries served us well for over seven years.

Many AGM batteries require yet another level of voltage, 14.2 to 14.3 volts. This allows some mild gassing to occur, which will be recombined into the sulfuric acid electrolyte as the battery charges. Table 9-2 summarizes charging voltages for each battery type.

CHARGING METHODS

There are three main charging methods—tapered, two-stage, and multistage—which we'll cover in the order of their development and prevalence.

Constant-Voltage, or Tapered, Charging

The most common charging method—but by no means the most suitable for RV deep-cycle house batteries—is called constant-voltage, or tapered, charging, and it is used with the following devices:

- automotive alternators
- portable generators with DC output

■ many converters with charging capability

■ most ordinary portable battery chargers

Tapered charging has been the standard charging method for years because it is simple and inexpensive. In your automobile and in its many other applications, it works like this:

1. The voltage source (alternator, charger, etc.) produces a specific voltage, ranging from 13.8 to 14.5 volts, which is applied to the battery. This voltage varies with the manufacturer (see the sidebar on charging rates on page 99).

2. Initially the discharged battery accepts a high-amperage current, which makes the battery voltage rise quickly. The current at that point can be as high as the maximum amps allowed by the charging device's rating (such as a 100 amp alternator, a 40 amp converter/charger, or a portable 50 amp charger).

3. Once the battery voltage reaches about 13.5 volts, the high-amperage output of the charge rapidly tapers off and stabilizes.

4. A voltage regulator on the charging device then allows the amperage flow to continue to taper off in order to maintain a constantly applied voltage until the battery is fully charged.

The battery voltage rises quickly at first because of the high voltage differential between the discharged battery and the charger. The surfaces of the battery plates are charged first, and this happens quickly. Then the charge has to diffuse to the interior of the plates, which happens at a much slower rate. Acceptance of the charge slows down, and the regulator starts to taper off the charging rate. So although the charging device has high-amperage output, it is only operating at this rate for a short time—basically until the surfaces of the plates have been fully charged. Given enough time, as the charge diffuses to the interior of the plates, the battery will eventually reach the applied voltage of the charger or alternator and be considered fully charged.

We have found that under the best of conditions, a large alternator of 100 amps or more may only charge at a maximum rate of 50% of its rating (in this case, 50 amps) for a few minutes or so during the beginning of the charge cycle. We once timed the charging rate of our Dodge truck's 136 amp alternator. With the batteries discharged to about 22%, the alternator initially put out 42.1 amps for about 10 minutes; then the charging rate started dropping. After another 30 minutes, the rate was down to 12.5 amps—not enough to quickly replace the 40 amp-hours the batteries had been discharged to (see Table 10-3). This charging rate would eventually charge the battery, but it would take 5 or more hours of charging and driving to do so. Naturally, these results will vary with different alternators.

Tapered charging works well for most normal automotive use. Usually the starting battery is only slightly discharged during the initial cranking of the engine, and tapered charging will quickly recharge it. Further electrical needs such as the ignition system, lights, radio, etc., are met by the alternator directly while the engine is running, not from the battery. However, this method is not really suited for recharging the deep-cycle house batteries of an RV, which (1) have thicker plates and a correspondingly slower diffusion rate, and (2) may be depleted by anywhere from 25% to 50% or more of the batteries' capacity. Tapered charging would likely result in undercharging or overcharging, depending on the charging time. Either way, it would shorten battery life. Tapered charging can be more efficient if the regulator holds the voltage higher for a longer period of time. See the results of the Iota charger/converter test, pages 118–19.

Two-Stage Charging

Another method that is becoming popular and is superior to tapered charging for recharging deep-cycle batteries is the two-stage process called constant amperage/constant voltage charging.

Studies have shown that heavily discharged deep-cycle batteries can accept a high-amperage charging rate of as much as 40% of the batteries' amp-hour capacity for a reasonable time. This is particularly true for gel-cell batteries. A 200 amp-hour gel-cell battery bank can handle an initial charging rate of up to 80 amps (200 Ah × 0.40 = 80 amps).

A two-stage regulator directs the charging device to maintain its maximum amperage output longer than it would in a constant-voltage process. For example, the regulator on a charger designed for this process and rated for 80 amps of constant output will deliver that 80 amps to the battery by letting the voltage begin low and slowly rise to the lower limits of charging.

By the time the charging voltage of any deep-cycle battery reaches the charger's maximum set-point output of between 14.0 and 14.4 volts, the battery has received approximately 70% of its full charge. Often this takes just minutes instead of the hours required with regular tapered charging. This first stage, the constant-amperage part of the charge, is called the *bulk charge stage*.

The second part of the process is called the *absorption*, or *acceptance*, *stage*. In this stage the set voltage that has now been reached is held at a constant rate, and the amperage is allowed to taper off as in the constant-voltage process. However, this whole process has been speeded up because of the high-amperage rate continuously applied at the beginning of the charge. The battery then accepts the charge at its own internal diffusion rate until it is fully charged.

Rule 5. For fast recharging of deep-cycle batteries, the constant amperage/constant voltage two-stage charging process is the best method.

Several types of charging equipment have two-stage charging options:

■ specially designed alternators and regulators
■ some converter/chargers

- some solar panel regulators

- the built-in chargers in most inverters

The equipment for two-stage charging is specifically designed to maintain the necessary high-amperage output. Standard alternators and chargers, even if equipped with a two-stage regulator, may not be able to handle the constant high-amperage output.

Multistage Charging

Multistage charging is also called smart charging because it is controlled by a regulator with a microprocessor that oversees the three (sometimes four) stages of this charging process, which are as follows:

- bulk stage (constant amperage)

- absorption, or acceptance, stage (constant voltage)

- float stage (a lower maintenance voltage)

- equalization stage (not used in all applications)

Many multistage regulators let you choose the specific type of battery you will be charging—flooded wet-cell, gel-cell, or AGM. Charging devices that are offered with multistage regulators include alternators, generators, chargers, and solar panels. Balmar (www.balmar.net) and Xantrex Technology (www.xantrex.com) are two leading suppliers of multistage regulators and battery chargers.

The first two stages proceed exactly as with the two-stage charging covered above. But then the regulator automatically switches to the float stage, which reduces the charging voltage to a constant low of 13.2 to 13.7. This

Charging Rates—What's Best

According to manufacturers, the very best way to charge batteries absent any considerations of time or effort would be at a low amperage rate of 5% of amp-hour capacity at 13.8 volts. This would allow the battery to accept the charge at its natural diffusion rate with light gassing, only slight heating, and minimal depletion of its electrolyte. The problem with this method—which is close to the traditional tapered-charge approach—is that it is simply impractical. You might need 10 to 20 hours of charging time to restore a battery to full capacity, and rarely do you have the luxury of that much charging time.

Another axiom is that the lower the rate of charge and the longer the length of time to reach the gassing voltage, the higher the state of charge in the battery. For example, if any completely discharged battery is continuously charged at an amperage that is 25% of its amp-hour capacity, it will take 2.75 hours to reach gassing voltage, at which time the battery will be charged to 70% of its capacity. But if deep-cycle wet-cell batteries (including 6-volt golf-cart batteries in series) are charged at a 40% rate, they will reach the gassing voltage level sooner, and at only 55% of capacity. But why is this so?

Because of the thicker plates in deep-cycle batteries, the diffusion rate of the acid through the battery is slower than the charge rate. This ultimately results in a lower state of charge. If charging is continued at the higher rate of 40%, excessive gassing and heating will occur with little additional charging. The charge rate must be reduced to about 25% of capacity in order for charging to continue to completion.

Gel-cell batteries can be charged at the higher rate of 40% because there is no diffusion of acid in the electrolyte to contend with, and these batteries have a high acceptance rate. However, gel-cell batteries often reach the charge voltage too quickly and thus trip a two-stage charger into its absorption stage before the battery has received the full bulk charge.

The best all-around compromise bulk-stage charging rate is 25% of the battery amp-hour rating. A lower rate will take too long, and a higher rate will result in a lower state of charge.

level of charging voltage maintains the battery at a full charge without causing gassing or overcharging. It also compensates for self-discharging by keeping the battery topped off.

Note: Although the lower voltage of 13.2 maintains the charge in the battery, it cannot handle additional loads—such as lights, water pumps, etc.—without discharging the battery. Maintenance devices, such as converters, usually operate at the slightly higher voltage of 13.7 volts to handle these loads.

The equalization, or conditioning, stage included on some charging devices is designed to rejuvenate wet-cell batteries. This stage applies a controlled high-voltage overcharge (up to as much as 16.2 volts) at low amperage (5% of amp-hour capacity or lower) to the battery for no more than 4 hours to bring the cells back to their fully charged states. The purpose is to equalize the voltage in all the battery's cells and remove excess sulfate from the cells' plates, and ideally it should be done every month or so.

This stage is only for golf-cart wet-cell and 12-volt deep-cycle wet-cell batteries. (You will have to top off with distilled water after this procedure.) *Do not* perform this stage on sealed AGM or gel-cell batteries. Check the manufacturer's instructions on how to perform this function. The only sure way to test for proper equalization is with a hydrometer (see Chapter 8), checking the cells repeatedly until all cells are up to full charge.

Multistage charging offers the speed and completeness of two-stage charging together with the possibility of maintaining float voltages and periodically equalizing the batteries.

Golf-Cart Batteries and Float Charging

A little-known problem with charging 6-volt golf-cart wet-cell batteries is that most golf-cart battery manufacturers do not recommend float charging, stating that these batteries are not designed for this type of continuous charging. Golf-cart batteries require a rest period between the charging and recharging cycles.

One manufacturer told us that although its golf-cart batteries could be float-charged, it preferred that floating not be used and that the batteries be rested after charging. But if the batteries were floated, it should be done at no more than 13.5 volts. Golf-cart batteries also have a high rate of self-discharge during such rest periods.

This requirement is something that does not necessarily fit in with the RV lifestyle, particularly that of fulltimers and snowbirds. These RVers may be at a campground for long periods of time with their RVs plugged into the campground's electric outlet, and using their converter/chargers or inverter/chargers to supply 12-volt power and to keep the batteries fully charged. It appears that only a few manufacturers of chargers and solar panel regulators are aware of this golf-cart battery requirement. We know of one multistage charger manufacturer and one solar panel regulator manufacturer that provide settings that will eliminate the float stage from the charging process. Until this Catch-22 is resolved, however, RVers recharging 6-volt golf-cart batteries with multistage regulators would do well to terminate charging after the absorption phase.

BATTERY LIFE CYCLES

All batteries have a life span based on the number of times the battery has been discharged and recharged; each discharge/recharge (D/R) represents one life cycle.

To illustrate, let's say we have an automotive SLI battery with an approximate life span of three years. In the course of a day, while driving around town, we start the engine four times, and the alternator recharges the battery after each start. This represents four D/R cycles per day. Multiplying the four cycles by 365 days per year for three years gives the battery a projected life span of 4,380 life cycles ($4 \times 365 \times 3 = 4,380$ life cycles).

Now let's look at deep-cycle battery usage. Usually a deep-cycle battery on an RV is discharged during the evening and recharged during the day, equaling one life cycle per day. With this in mind, a three-year deep-cycle battery would have a theoretical life span of 1,095 life cycles ($365 \times 3 = 1,095$ life cycles).

Unfortunately, other factors also affect the number of life cycles. The depth of discharge (DOD) and the frequency of deep discharges can drastically shorten the life of the battery. Here are some examples:

- Discharging a standard deep-cycle wet-cell battery to 50% of its amp-hour capacity will give it a life span of about 1,000 cycles if it is well maintained.

- Limiting the depth of discharge to 10% of amp-hour capacity will increase the battery's life span to as much as 20,000 cycles.

- Occasional discharges to a depth of 80% can reduce the life span to as little as 200 to 300 life cycles.

Golf-cart, gel-cell, and AGM batteries have a longer life span than ordinary deep-cycle batteries. Six-volt golf-cart batteries can occasionally be discharged to a depth of 60% to 80% because of their heavier, thicker plates without too much ill effect. Good-quality gel-cells can go to a DOD of about 60% without damage. The effects of DOD on AGM batteries are still not yet completely known. We must, however, ask ourselves if we really want—or need—to discharge our batteries to a depth as great as 60% to 80%, pushing them to their limits.

It is easy to see why it is smart to keep the DOD as low as possible, because it will definitely increase the battery's life span. It is wiser, and perhaps cheaper in the long run, to have a larger battery bank to handle large amp-hour demands than it is to overdischarge a smaller bank of batteries. If you regularly discharge your battery bank by about 100 amp-hours, your 200 amp-hour bank would be down 50%. If you increased your bank size to 400 amp-hours, then the same amount of discharge would only bring the batteries down by 25%.

It is good practice never to discharge batteries by more than 50% of capacity. We know of one independent authority and several manufacturers who suggest limiting DOD to only 20%, and another authority who recommends only 33.3%. Our own practice and recommendation is to try to hold DOD to no more than 25% of amp-hour capacity as much as possible.

Rule 6. Do not discharge batteries to more than 25% of Ah capacity if at all possible.

Even though golf-cart and gel-cell batteries can handle deep discharges, the fact that you must be able to recharge them the next day is a compelling reason to restrict the depth of discharge as much as possible.

Rule 7. Never discharge your batteries to more than your charging equipment's capability
to recharge them within the next daily charge period. (Unlike the other rules,
this one is based more on common sense than empirical evidence.)

If you discharge a 200 amp-hour bank by 80% of its amp-hour capacity, the batteries will be down 160 amp-hours. Your charging equipment must be capable of putting back this many amp-hours and more during the next charge period. Because of inefficiencies in the charging process, for every amp-hour consumed, 1.2 amp-hours must be returned to the battery. A battery bank that is down 160 amp-hours must have 192 amp-hours put back the next day for a full recharge.

If you do a little math, you can easily see how difficult or even impossible it would be to achieve that level of charging the next day. Here are some options:

- Suppose you have two 100-watt solar panels capable of delivering about 10 amps in full sunshine. It would require 19.2 hours of continuous charging at full panel output to completely recharge the batteries (10 amps × 19.2 hours = 192 amp-hours). But you will rarely if ever have 19 hours of full sunshine. You could get more panels, but they would probably be more than could fit on the roof of your RV.

- A 100 amp engine alternator with a standard regulator working at 50% efficiency would require an equal duration of driving time (19 hours) to recharge, and that doesn't sound like much fun!

- An alternator with a multistage regulator or a multistage charger powered by a 120 VAC generator would probably do the job in 4 hours or more. The question then becomes, do you really want to run your engine or generator for such a long period just to charge your batteries?

To us, it makes more sense simply to limit the size of your discharges to no more than 25% of amp-hour capacity and be able to comfortably recharge your batteries the next day.

Rule 8. Always fully recharge the batteries after each deep discharge. Allow some resting time of
the batteries between cycles if possible.

You should always fully recharge your batteries after each deep discharge. If you only partially recharge your batteries between discharge cycles, your battery life will be diminished. Cycles where the battery is discharged down to, say, 50% of amp-hour capacity and then recharged to only 80% of capacity should be avoided at all costs. If the charging system cannot fully recharge the batteries, such deep discharges should definitely be avoided.

We have mentioned previously the need to rest batteries as much as possible between charging and discharging. The human body can be compared with a battery. We humans work and play hard, using a lot of energy. We then refuel our bodies by eating, and after awhile we have to rest or sleep. Batteries work the same way: they put out a lot of energy during discharge, and are then recharged, but they need to rest too. Resting for a battery is just as important as recharging and the proper maintenance.

As matter of fact, most manufacturers recommend allowing batteries to rest for 24 hours after recharging. This is rather impractical for boondocking RVers, since they need to use their batteries more frequently than that. But a few hours of rest will work wonders in adding to the life of your batteries.

Rule 9. Rest your batteries as much as possible.

To explain further, as a battery is discharged, the cell nearest to the terminal through which the current flows will have a lower voltage than the terminal at the other end of the battery. Conversely, when a battery is recharged, the cell nearest the charging current terminal will develop a higher voltage than its neighbors, and the one farthest from the current will be the lowest. This higher recharging voltage is called *surface voltage*. Resting allows the surface voltage to dissipate throughout the other cells and equalize the overall voltage. So voltage readings will not be accurate unless the battery has been allowed to rest first.

We make it a habit to rest our batteries. To accomplish this we've wired our converter/charger and the charger in the inverter to the same AC circuit with a 30 amp, two-way, double-pole/double-throw switch. The switch allows us to select whichever charging device we want to use, and putting the switch toggle in the middle position turns off both devices. Whenever we leave the trailer, we turn off both devices, allowing the batteries to rest. Even when we're home during the day, we shut off all charging devices if they are not needed. This has extended our batteries' lives. We had a pair of cheap deep-cycle 12-volt batteries that lasted for five years, and they were still going strong when we got the chance to buy two gel-cell batteries at a good price. Those in turn lasted seven years with no sign of failure, at which point we sold the trailer.

THE RULE OF TWENTY-FIVES

Perhaps you've noticed we've mentioned 25% of amp-hour capacity frequently and in different contexts. Here's a summary that we call the Rule of Twenty-Fives:

1. **Do not apply a load to the batteries greater than 25% of amp-hour capacity—except for short periods.** We recommend limiting loads to 25% because greater loads will reduce the amp-hour capacity of your batteries. This percentage also plays an important part in inverter size and operation.

2. **Do not regularly discharge batteries by more than 25% of their amp-hour capacity.** Holding to a 25% depth of discharge will allow faster recharging, protect the battery bank from overdischarging, and give the battery more life cycles. Occasional discharges to a depth of 50% are acceptable provided that you allow sufficient charging time to bring the battery back to a complete charge.

3. **Always recharge at a rate of about 25% of amp-hour capacity.** We recommend recharging at a rate of 25% amp-hour capacity (through the bulk charging phase) because this is the best overall rate of charge. It will give a fast recharge yet also allow the batteries to reach their fullest charge. If batteries have been deeply discharged, higher rates can be used for even faster times, as long as the charging method allows for an automatic reduction after 75% of the charge has been completed from the higher amperage rate to the 25% rate. If it doesn't, stick to the 25% rate overall.

Working within these guidelines will result in longer battery life, higher battery capacity, faster battery recharging, and happier boondock camping.

CHARGING DEVICES

In the final chapters of the book, we will cover the various charging devices and technologies:

Chapter 10: Engine alternators

Chapter 11: Generators, converters/chargers, and inverters

Chapter 12: Solar panels and wind generators

If you recall our fictional couple from Chapter 1, Bob and Mary Jones used several methods throughout their two-week trip to charge their batteries: the alternator when driving, solar panels when camping, the generator when the neighbors were gone, and a wind generator on a bluff overlooking a beach. Each device has advantages and disadvantages, and no one method will fully supply all your charging needs all of the time. Understanding each method, identifying your family's pattern of battery use, and taking into account how long you'd like to boondock will help you design a balanced system.

CHAPTER 10

Engine Alternators

An alternator is a machine that generates electricity by spinning a magnet (the rotor) inside a series of coils (the stator). The resulting power output is AC current, which is changed (rectified) to DC current via silicon diodes. It is coupled with a voltage regulator that controls the rate of electrical current into the battery or batteries to prevent over- or undercharging. (For a more detailed explanation of alternators, see our book *RV Electrical Systems*.)

ALTERNATORS AND RVS

In your everyday car, SUV, or truck, the alternator keeps the engine, or SLI, battery charged. Its amperage output is just high enough to replace the current used to start the engine, then it tapers off quickly until it has little charging capability. When your truck is attached to a trailer or the vehicle is a motorhome, the alternator has the additional task of charging the house batteries. In fact, for many years the engine alternator was the *only* way to charge the

(RVIA)

house battery. This system worked reasonably well because the demand for electrical energy from the house battery was small; usually a few lights were used in the evening, along with a radio (which may even have had its own internal batteries), so the RV battery was only discharged by a few amp-hours. The alternator very likely, and probably without too much trouble, fully charged the battery the next day while the RVers were traveling to their next destination.

Modern RVs, however, have more equipment and appliances that require more power and larger battery banks. They now have charging requirements that some stock engine alternators are not capable of handling. But today's alternators and regulators have gone through their own transformation. So it is now possible to upgrade your charging system and improve the capabilities of its alternator.

One way to upgrade is to install a multistage voltage regulator on your alternator. The standard regulator is a constant-voltage regulator, and so provides a tapered charge. It will not do a good job of rapidly recharging deeply discharged batteries. But note that the alternator cannot have an internal regulator (which are usually found in stock alternators).

If one of these new regulators will not fit your engine, then it is possible to replace your stock alternator with a high-output alternator. A multistage alternator will certainly improve the charging rate of your batteries, and it may be a less expensive way to get this modern means of charging than some of the other high-powered charging systems.

A modern high-output alternator. (Wrangler NW Power Products)

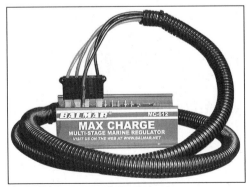

A multistage regulator. (Balmar)

Another advantage of a high-output alternator is that it can handle running your onboard inverter during travel, allowing you to use high-wattage AC equipment. (Although this will probably not include an air conditioner, even though we have heard stories of RVers doing just this. It is just too large a load.)

The alternator will still have to be capable of handling other extra electrical loads. These loads can help steal away horsepower from your engine for hill climbing and such, but the alternator load is still a very small one for large pickup truck and motorhome engines—1 horsepower for every 50 amps of electrical power.

Installing a multistage regulator can present problems with the onboard computer on your engine, however, and it may even void the warranty on your vehicle. Also, it could interfere with the diagnostic computer in your local auto repair shop. The bottom line is that this is not an easy do-it-yourself project. You must be knowledgeable about automotive systems and have the necessary test equipment. We recommend hiring someone who knows how to wire this equipment. We have worked with Wrangler NW Power Products (www.wranglernw.com) for years, which specializes in solving these sorts of charging problems.

VOLTAGE DROP

If you have a standard tapered alternator, you may be able to improve its charging capabilities by checking that it's wired properly. The use of an inadequately sized wire can result in voltage drop between the alternator and batteries, which can greatly diminish your alternator's charging capabilities.

Voltage drop is a loss in voltage in a circuit; that is, voltage is lost between the power source—such as the alternator—and the load—for our purposes, the battery bank. The cause is high electrical resistance. Some materials conduct electricity very well (known as conductors), and some do not (known as insulators). All conductors resist the flow of current to some degree. Even copper wire, the metal found in all automotive and RV wiring, has some resistance. Resistance in a charge wire can cause voltage drop, especially over a long wire run. Also, as the diameter of a wire decreases, the amount of current it can carry (its *ampacity*) also decreases.

Voltage drop will not only affect battery charging but also the performance of your appliances and equipment because they won't be receiving enough power to run properly. This is why choosing the correct wire size is so important when wiring a circuit. Basically, increasing the diameter of the wire will reduce voltage drop.

As to what size wire to use, fortunately there are tables that will help us with that process, such as Table 10-1 on page 108.

Here's an example. At 50 amps, 14-gauge wire has a voltage drop of 5.16 volts over a run of 40 feet (20 feet for the positive wire and 20 feet for the negative wire). This is the usual combined distance of most charge lines for travel and fifth-wheel trailers. With this much voltage drop, the voltage reaching your batteries would be only 9.34 volts, lower than the

Table 10-1. Wire Ampacity and Voltage Drop						
		Voltage Drop per Foot @				
Wire Size	Ampacity[1]	25 Amps	50 Amps	100 Amps	150 Amps	200 Amps
3/0	225	0.00157	0.00315	0.00630	0.00945	0.01260
2/0	195	0.00198	0.00397	0.00795	0.01192	0.01590
1/0	170	0.00250	0.00500	0.01000	0.01500	0.02000
1	150	0.00315	0.00630	0.01260	0.01890	0.02520
2	130	0.00397	0.00795	0.01590	0.02385	0.03180
4	95	0.00632	0.01265	0.02530	0.03795	0.05060
6	75	0.01006	0.02015	0.04030	NP[2]	NP
8	55	0.01602	0.03205	0.06410	NP	NP
10	30	0.02550	0.05100	NP	NP	NP
12	25	0.04050	0.08100	NP	NP	NP
14	20	0.06450	NP	NP	NP	NP
16	10	NP	NP	NP	NP	NP

1. The maximum recommended amperage for the wire size.
2. NP = Not Practical or safe to use because of too much voltage drop.

voltage of a dead battery. Note that 14-gauge wire is suited only for lights and light loads. Its ampacity is only 20 amps, which means that loads over 20 amps will cause voltage drop.

Or say we increase the wire size to 12-gauge wire, keeping the same amperage and wire run. Now the voltage drop per foot would be 0.08100: 40 feet × 0.081 = 3.4 volts, which is still quite a loss. It's easy to see why battery charging can be greatly curtailed by voltage drop.

How much voltage drop is allowable? Table 10-2 lists some examples. At 14 volts, the usual minimum charging voltage for a 1% drop should not exceed 0.14 volt; at 12 volts the drop should not be more than 0.12 volt. A 1% maximum drop is the best for charging lines to get the greatest charge possible. For purposes other than charging, a drop of 3% is permissible—0.36 volt at 12 volts.

When we first became fulltimers, our alternator could not satisfactorily charge the batteries on our 23-foot travel trailer. We suspected that the problem was voltage drop in the charge line between the alternator and the batteries. After charging the batteries via another source, we did a voltage check with the engine running. The voltage at the alternator was 13.8 volts, but only 13.2 volts at the batteries, showing a definite voltage drop. With further checking, we found that

Table 10-2. Acceptable Voltage Drop		
Allowable Voltage Drop (%)	Volts	Charging Voltage
1	14	0.14
1	13	0.13
1	12	0.12
3	14	0.42
3	13	0.39
3	12	0.36

the wiring harness, which was part of the manufacturer's towing package on our truck, used 14-gauge wire for the charge line, while the rest of the line—that was installed by the dealer—was 12-gauge wire. The whole line was about 14 feet in length and used a ground wire to the chassis. No wonder the voltage was so low.

After we discovered our voltage drop problem, we had three options: increase the size of the charging line, switch to a high-output alternator with a multistage regulator, or do both. We chose to increase the size of the charging line. We thought 8-gauge would be about the right size. So we made the rounds of auto-parts and RV dealers looking for 8-gauge wire. One RV dealer asked what we wanted with wire that large. When we told him, he replied, "Any size wire will do the job." Later, we laughed at the man's ignorance, but in retrospect, he was partially right because voltage will equalize eventually over many hours.

Since most stock alternators produce a tapered charge delivering its maximum amperage at low voltage, the high-amperage output never reaches the battery because of the voltage drop, but as the amperage output diminishes, eventually a charge will reach the battery. So smaller wire will charge the battery over a long period of time (although you should never use anything less than 4-gauge wire for charge lines), but the high-amperage output is lost in the process, particularly when fast charging is desirable.

On our present fifth-wheel trailer, we use 4-gauge wire (with welding wire plugs so we can break the connection when we unhitch the pickup truck). It has dramatically improved the charging rate. When the batteries are fully charged, we now find that the voltage is the same at both the alternator and the batteries—no loss. Admittedly, it still takes 4, 5, or more hours of charging to bring the batteries to a full charge, but they will get charged when we are traveling. When we spend several days at a campsite, running the engine for 30 to 60 minutes at a higher rpm than idle helps speed up charging when the sky is cloudy and the solar panels need some help. It does come at a high price, considering the cost of gasoline and diesel fuel. However, the combination of these two charging sources (alternator and solar panels) will charge batteries faster than either will by itself because of the additive nature of the two processes. This is particularly true after the high-amperage alternator output has tapered down to a few amps.

Trailers usually present the most problems while charging due to the long wire runs between the alternator and the batteries, which can lead to voltage drop. Motorhomes do not have this problem because their batteries are usually very close to the alternator. However, we have seen some motorhomes with wiring problems as bad as those on trailers. Far too often manufacturers will install the batteries wherever there is sufficient room for them, not where they will be the most efficient or effective. We once saw a diesel-pusher motorhome at an RV show where the house batteries were located at the front of the rig behind the grille. We measured the distance, and it was more than 30 feet one way. So, figuring on twice the distance, that would mean a run of about 65 feet, and the wire was only 10-gauge, causing voltage drop of about 3.31 volts. RVers should investigate prospective RVs for wiring irregularities before buying them, or they may find they have a large rewiring job to do.

TESTING ALTERNATOR EFFICIENCY

Table 10-3 shows the results of a test we conducted with our 136 amp truck alternator. We discharged our batteries until they were down 47 amp-hours according to our amp-hour meter, which was a discharge of 29.3% of capacity. The battery voltage was 12.4 volts. The next morning we left on a trip of 122 miles to our next destination where we would be staying in a campground with full hookups. Here are some highlights of the test:

- We started the engine and waited for the engine to reach operating voltage. Then we plugged in the separate trailer charge line. Immediately the charging amperage rose to 42.1 amps, the battery voltage to 12.9 volts.

- After 10 minutes, the charging amperage had dropped to 15.8 amps, and the voltage had risen to 13.4 volts.

- After 30 minutes, the charging amperage was 12.5, and the voltage had stabilized at 13.6 volts.

- After 3 hours and 10 minutes of driving, we arrived at our destination. The charging amperage was at 7.5 amps, and the battery voltage had risen to 13.7 volts. But our amp-hour meter showed that we still had 15.5 amp-hours to replenish for a full charge.

- At the campground, our converter/charger completed the charging cycle.

- We projected the alternator would have needed another 2 hours of driving time to finishing charging the batteries, making a total of 5 hours and 10 minutes.

As you can see, alternator tapered charging can involve many hours of driving, although it will do a fairly good job, in part thanks to the 4-gauge charging wire we installed.

The charging time would have been much longer in our older trucks, which had smaller alternators than our present one. You may wonder why such a large alternator didn't do a better job. First, the alternator has to provide all the electrical needs of the engine, including the dash air conditioner, lights, radio, and so forth, so there is less electrical energy left for charging. Second, most standard stock alternators are only about 50% efficient. And third, with the Dodge Cummins diesel, when the engine and outside temperatures are about freezing—the precise time when you wish to charge batteries as fast as possible—the alternator

Table 10-3. Test of Our 136 Amp Alternator			
Time	Charging Amps	Amp-Hour Reading	Voltage
9:00 a.m.	42.1	−47.0	12.9
9:10 a.m.	15.8	−44.5	13.4
9:30 a.m.	12.5	−41.0	13.6
10:00 a.m.	11.9	−34.7	13.6
10:30 a.m.	11.3	−29.5	13.6
11:00 a.m.	9.6	−24.5	13.6
11:30 a.m.	8.0	−20.8	13.6
12:10 p.m.	7.5	−15.5	13.7

must provide the power to recharge the 90 amps the intake manifold heater draws from the truck batteries during start-up.

But to sum up, the alternator as a charging device can do a reasonably good job if the amp-hour deficit is not too large and you use an adequately sized wire for the charge line.

The consumption of electrical power by today's cars and trucks is tremendous considering the need to power air conditioners, heaters, radios, CD players, and the addition of many new electronic components used by RV or truck systems. There is even talk of increasing automotive electrical power to anything from 24-volt to 40-volt systems. This of course would have a huge effect on RVing. It would mean changes in converters, inverters, batteries, chargers, and alternators, as well as the electrical systems within the RV itself. However, at the present time it is all a rumor that may never happen.

BATTERY SWITCHES, ISOLATORS, AND COMBINERS

Up to now we've focused on the alternator in relation to the house battery. But there is another battery involved in this system, the SLI battery, which is also connected to the alternator. Unless it is isolated from the house battery, the SLI battery will be discharged as the house battery is being used. We can resolve this potential problem with three different types of devices: battery switches, battery isolators, and battery combiners.

Battery Switches

A marine battery switch is one way to separate the house battery bank from the SLI battery in a motorhome. If you are knowledgeable, you can install one yourself. It has settings that allow you to switch from one battery to another. When discharging, set the switch so only the

house battery bank is accessed; during charging, switch to the setting that allows both to be charged at the same time. This system works great—as long as you remember to change the switch to the proper setting!

Unfortunately, battery switches do not work with tow vehicles and trailers because the switch must be turned to the engine battery for normal operation.

Battery Isolators

A second and more convenient method of separating the SLI and house batteries is with an isolator, either a solid-state diode isolator or a mechanical-relay isolator.

Diode isolators allow current to flow in only one direction; in this case, from the

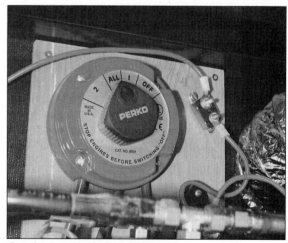

Our battery switch, which we have only for safety. We can turn off all the batteries, which you can't do in most trailers.

alternator to each of the two battery banks, but not toward each other. The battery bank that needs the charge will receive it, and the other one will reject it. This isolator works well with both motorhomes and tow vehicles for trailers.

The mechanical-relay, or solenoid, isolator is activated by the vehicle's ignition switch. When you turn on the ignition, the solenoid closes an electromagnetic switch that connects the SLI battery to the alternator circuit. The battery is connected to the alternator (and thus able to be charged) only when the ignition switch is in the On position. When the switch is turned off, the solenoid springs back, breaking the connection, thereby protecting the SLI battery from being drained as the house battery is being used.

Each type of isolator has disadvantages. The solid-state diode isolator creates a voltage drop across the diode of as much as 0.6 volt or more. The alternator must deliver a higher voltage to compensate for the loss, which overworks it. Also the diode isolator can become very hot during use, so it must be mounted on a heat sink, which dissipates the heat.

When selecting a diode isolator, make sure it is rated at a higher amperage than your alternator so the diodes don't burn out. For example, use a 150 amp isolator with a 125 amp alternator.

The mechanical-relay isolator uses a spring-loaded switch, and the springs can wear out and break, although they are quite easy to replace.

When we purchased a new truck for our tow vehicle, we were dismayed to learn there was absolutely no room under the hood for installing an isolator. We were very perplexed by this, and finally decided to just attach the charging line to the alternator wire at the battery along with the engine battery wire. This has worked for us because we have a trailer, but it would not work if we had a motorhome because the engine battery is always connected to the house batteries. We must, however, remember to disconnect both the battery-charging line and the regular trailer connection plugs before we do any boondock camping or we could discharge the engine battery.

Battery Combiners

The latest type of protection for all battery banks is a battery combiner. Combiners electronically connect up to three battery banks to any charging source. After charging is complete, and the voltage drops to a preset voltage, the combiner disconnects the banks from each other. Basically, a combiner comprises two or more solenoid-operated relays with a sophisticated electronic control regulator, which makes it more than just an isolator.

The advantage of this system is that you can adjust the combiner so the turn-on and turn-off voltages are appropriate for charging either AGM, gel-cell, or wet-cell batteries. Additionally, you can use a combiner with any charging source: alternators, solar panels, shore-power chargers, and wind generators, or in combination. This makes them very useful for controlling charging systems on both motorhomes and truck/trailers.

CHAPTER 11

Generators, Converters/ Chargers, and Inverters

In this chapter, we'll cover three more charging technologies: generators, converters/chargers, and inverters. Each device can be purchased with or without chargers, although you should have at least one with charging capabilities, and each performs a different function for the RVer. A generator produces 120-volt AC power. A converter changes 120-volt AC power to 12-volt DC power. When boondocking, a converter/charger connected to a generator can charge your batteries. An inverter converts 12-volt DC power to 120-volt DC power, which is useful when boondocking and you want to run a 120-volt appliance.

(RVIA)

GENERATORS

Generators are standard equipment in motorhomes, and are usually used for running the air conditioner while traveling. Although fuel prices can make it a more expensive option, a generator will get the job done. You can use your batteries at night and recharge them during the day with the generator, while also running an appliance or two. We do find it strange that not many motorhomers boondock since a generator makes a motorhome the best-equipped RV for boondocking and provides the easiest way to begin boondocking. But most boondockers tend to be trailerists, who must go to great lengths to equip their rigs for easy boondocking.

Types of Generators

RVers can use either a large, built-in generator called genset, or a smaller portable generator.

Gensets

Gensets are usually installed in motorhomes, although they can be mounted in storage lockers of large trailers. A genset is either hard-wired into the RV's 120-volt AC system or accessed via an outlet where a shore-power cable can be plugged in. Most installations allow you to activate the genset by throwing a switch.

With a genset, you can have access to a high-kilowatt output, which can range from 2.5 to 17 kilowatts (2,500 watts to 17,000 watts). With this much power, you not only have all the advantages of a campground hookup, but also quite a bit of battery-charging capability if you have a good battery charger.

Because they are built in, and powered by a combustion engine, gensets must have adequate ventilation and exhaust systems to prevent a buildup of fumes and carbon monoxide in the RV (see Chapter 6 for more on carbon monoxide).

A genset is a very satisfactory way to charge your batteries when boondocking. While the batteries are charging, you also have current available for other purposes: cooking supper in the microwave, running the vacuum cleaner, answering e-mail, or cooling things down with the air conditioner. Also, charging with a genset is more efficient than running or driving your motorhome so the alternator can charge the batteries, and is more cost effective given the cost of fuel. When coupled with a multistage charger, a genset is as efficient at charging batteries as a high-output alternator with a multistage regulator.

The genset should have enough capacity to run all the items you wish to run at the same time. Manufacturers will often install a genset large enough to run the air conditioner, but no additional items. Before buying an RV, to make sure the genset is large enough add up the wattage of all the items you wish to run at one time; the wattage of the genset should be 20% larger than that amount.

Recently a new genset called the JuiceBox came on the market for trailer use. Manufactured by Onan (www.onan.com), it is a standard genset of adequate size (4,000 watts, which is just enough to power an air conditioner) that is mounted on the back bumper of the trailer in its own box. This is a handy location because you don't lose valuable locker space to the generator. The box is weatherproof and detachable, so you can remove it easily and set it up for use at the campsite or at home.

Portable Generators

Portable generators range in size from small 600-watt (0.6 kW) units to not-so-portable 4,000- to 5,000-watt (4 kW to 5 kW) units. A small portable generator is very useful, especially if you are an RVer with a small rig. You can use them to run low-wattage televisions, VCRs, DVD players, satellite receivers, and computers, as well as other appliances, providing the generator can handle the load (see below). Unfortunately, most portable units are not large enough to run an air conditioner.

For several years we used a 1,850-watt portable Coleman generator. It did a good job, but it could run only one appliance (such as a toaster or coffeemaker) at a time, and it was quite noisy.

Portable generators have two wattage ratings for their output power, the surge rating and the constant or continuous rating. The surge rating refers to the amount of momentary power available for starting compressors and certain electrical motors. The constant wattage rating refers to the maximum power available for continuous operation of appliances and tools. This rating is the one to consider for battery charging and other appliances that will be used for any length of time.

Selecting the Right Generator

In Chapter 8, we outlined a process for determining daily power consumption. You can use this same process to ensure you don't overload your generator, especially if it is on the small side. You want to be sure your wattage use doesn't surpass your generator's constant rating. For example, you cannot run a 1,200-watt hair dryer off a 600-watt generator or you would burn out the generator.

Table 8-3 lists the amps and watts of different appliances and equipment. As you create your own table or list of devices you use in your RV to determine amp-hour use, also incorporate the watts you use. This way you have a handy reference to look at when you want to run several appliances at the same time off your generator. After awhile, you'll learn what you can and can't run at the same time, but in the beginning you may find this method helpful. This list will also help you choose a generator that will meet your needs. For battery charging, the generator should be 1,000 watts or larger.

Staying Safe: Generator Backfires

If you plan to camp in USFS campgrounds and you buy a portable generator, make sure it has an exhaust manifold that has a backfire flame arrester to prevent starting a forest fire. Generators can backfire, which produces sparks, and the flame arrester will prevent this from happening. In fact, a flame arrester is a good idea for camping in any wilderness area, so make sure you buy a generator with a flame arrester.

Disadvantages

Generators are useful to have around, but they do have some drawbacks. All generators produce noise, although some with better mufflers are quieter than others. Many campgrounds have strict rules regarding generator use for this reason. Some parks prohibit their use altogether, and others restrict the times they may be used. Most people hate the noise of one running in the next site, not to mention the smell of the exhaust fumes. So be sure to consider your neighbors in your use of a generator. No one likes to be in a wilderness area and have the wonderful sound of the wind and the birds ruined by the noise of a generator.

Generators produce carbon monoxide. You should never go to sleep with a generator running. Fumes can enter the RV through windows or cracks. We covered carbon monoxide in Chapter 6, so refer back there for more information. With generators, however, you are not just endangering yourself. If you have neighbors camped close enough, they can be affected by carbon monoxide from your generator as well, particularly if they have their windows open.

Small generators may also produce current with voltage spikes that can affect the operation of sophisticated electronic equipment, such as a multistage battery charger—the very item that can be most useful to boondockers. Most charger manufacturers recommend using a portable generator of at least 1,000 watts of continuous output for multistage charging. Most manufacturers of inverters with built-in battery chargers recommend using a 2,000-watt portable generator.

CONVERTERS AND BATTERY CHARGERS

A converter is basically a step-down transformer. It lowers 120 VAC to 12 VAC, then rectifies it to DC voltage using diodes in a rectifier circuit. If this sounds familiar, it's because an alternator works in a similar way. In the early days of RVing, a converter was primarily used to provide 12-volt power to run the cabin lights when you were in a campground with an electrical hookup. This prevented the batteries from being discharged when a hookup was available. It did not charge the batteries; it was only an electrical substitute for battery usage.

Eventually chargers were incorporated into these units, but they only had a small amperage output, 3 to 8 amps, and were used to keep the battery topped off at full charge. They didn't have the ability to recharge a deeply discharged battery or battery bank. Some units were still basic converters, but by plugging in a Charge Wizard, an inexpensive adapter made by Progressive Dynamics, they could be converted into full-amperage chargers. These were good units, and we often wondered why RV manufacturers didn't spend the extra $30 and install such devices at the factory.

This is our old MagneTek converter mounted in our RV.

Most good-quality RVs manufactured today come equipped with built-in converter/chargers that have outputs ranging from 30 to 75 or more amps and using either tapered or multistage charging.

Types of Converters

When shopping for a converter/charger, you'll find a variety of types and options available—from basic to high tech. To give you an idea of the options, we'll describe two high-tech converter/chargers and a basic, low-end converter. Later we'll walk you through some tests we ran on two converter/chargers to give you an idea of performance and efficiency.

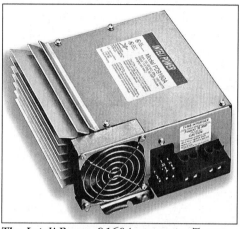

The Inteli-Power 9160A converter. To use it as a charger, you must plug in the Charge Wizard. (Progressive Dynamics)

The DLS-55 from Iota Engineering (www.iotaengineering.com) has a rating of 55 amps and provides multistage charging with the IQ Smart Controller. The Smart Controller automatically controls the bulk, absorption, and float stages according to the battery's capacity. It also monitors the battery at all times. Iota reports that its DLS converters produce exceptionally clean DC output, with little to no AC ripple (which can adversely affect AM radios, with effects ranging from static to failure).

Progressive Dynamics (www.progressivedyn.com) produces a new series of converter/chargers that incorporates the Charge Wizard adapter mentioned earlier. The bottom right

The Iota DLS-55 charger. (Iota Engineering)

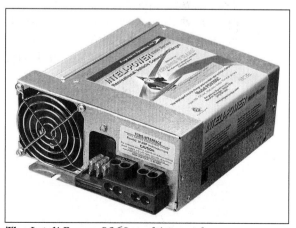

The Inteli-Power 9260 multistage charger. (Progressive Dynamics)

photo on page 117 shows the PD9260C converter/charger, rated at 60 amps. The built-in Charge Wizard provides automatic multistage charging.

In addition, both of the above models offer protection against low AC current, AC spikes, reverse polarity, and overheating.

While we've made the case more than once regarding the efficiency and speed of multistage charging, it is especially useful if you use a generator to power your converter/charger. The faster your batteries charge, the less generator time you use, which translates into less fuel consumed and shorter periods of extra noise.

Multistage chargers are available as stand-alone units as well as an option in many large inverters.

If your charging needs are small, an unregulated converter/charger will be just fine. A Sears battery charger will provide tapered charging using constant amperage, sometimes as low as 10 amps. Battery charging will be slow compared to multistage charging, but the job will get done. Remember, because this is an unregulated charger, you will have to constantly monitor the voltage to avoid overcharging. We tested a tapered converter/charger from Iota and have included the results below.

One problem with the chargers of this type is that they usually operate at 14 volts or higher. At this voltage, 12-volt lightbulbs have a very short life, and other 12-volt appliances may also not be designed to operate on this high voltage. Many of the better-quality units have the capability to drop this high voltage to a float voltage of 13.5 to 13.7 volts after the batteries are fully charged, thus protecting the life of lightbulbs and other appliances. Sometimes these chargers are only set at a low charging voltage of 13.8 volts or so to avoid this problem.

Converter/Charger Tests

We recently tested two converter/chargers: one was a good-quality tapered unit rated at 45 amps, and the other was a multistage unit rated at 40 amps.

Test 1: Iota 45 Amp Tapered Charger

The first test was with an older model Iota 45 amp charger powered through a campground outlet. We discharged our batteries over two evenings to −44.7 amp-hours (25.9% DOD). Here are the highlights from the test:

- The unit immediately delivered 46.7 amps. The voltage of the batteries was 13.5 volts.

- After 10 minutes, the amperage dropped to 29.6 amps as the voltage rose to 14 volts.

- After 1 hour, the amperage was down to 22.2 amps and the voltage remained at 14 volts. The amp-hour reading on the meter was −20.6 Ah.

- After 2 hours, the amperage was 10.9 amps, the voltage was 14.2, and the amp-hour reading was −7.2 Ah.

- After 3 hours, 21 minutes, the amperage was 3.2 amps, voltage was 14.2, and the amp-hour reading was 00.0. This was with a tapered-type charger that is far superior to most other chargers.

Test 2: Truecharge 40 Amp Multistage Charger

The second test was with a Truecharge 40 amp multistage charger also powered through a campground outlet. We discharged the batteries to −47.5 amp-hours (29.6% DOD). This test showed some interesting results:

- When we turned on the charger, it immediately produced 43.7 amps and held that output for 10 minutes while the battery voltage rose rapidly from 12.2 volts to 13.9 volts.

Table 11-1. Test of Iota 45 Amp Tapered Charger			
Time	Charging Amps	Amp-Hour Reading	Voltage
8:00 a.m.	46.7	−44.7	13.5
8:05 a.m.	31.2	−42.7	14.0
8:10 a.m.	29.6	−40.6	14.0
8:15 a.m.	30.2	−38.5	14.0
8:30 a.m.	30.1	−31.4	14.0
8:45 a.m.	25.7	−25.7	14.0
9:00 a.m.	22.2	−20.6	14.0
9:15 a.m.	18.2	−16.1	14.1
9:30 a.m.	15.2	−12.6	14.1
9:45 a.m.	12.8	−9.5	14.1
10:00 a.m.	10.9	−7.2	14.2
10:15 a.m.	9.3	−5.2	14.2
10:30 a.m.	8.0	−3.6	14.2
10:45 a.m.	5.3	−2.2	14.2
11:00 a.m.	4.4	−1.2	14.2
11:15 a.m.	3.5	−0.3	14.2
11:21 a.m.	3.2	0.0	14.2

Notes: The charger restored 24.1 Ah in the first hour, and 13.4 Ah in the second hour.

Battery voltage reached 14 volts in 5 minutes of charging.

3 hours and 21 minutes were required to recharge the batteries to full capacity, which is a good, fast charge.

- This rapid rise in voltage caused the charger to trip to the second stage, the acceptance stage, and the amperage tapered off to 25.3 amps.

- After 1 hour, the amperage was down to 22.9 amps, the amp-hour meter showed −23.5 Ah, and the voltage was still 13.9 volts. During the first hour the charger repeatedly recycled to a higher amperage output (this is normal for this type charger), which helped effect a faster charge.

- After 1½ hours, the voltage was at 14 volts.

- The amp-hour meter registered 00.0 after 3 hours and 47 minutes. The Truecharge fully charged the batteries 48 minutes faster than the Iota, and this was with a slightly larger (by 3.7 amp-hours) DOD.

We called the manufacturer about how quickly the charger switched to the acceptance stage. We were told that the charger was rated at a higher amperage than our battery bank

Testing our multistage Truecharge 40 amp charger.

Table 11-2. Charging Test of Truecharge 40 Amp Multistage Charger

Time	Charging Amps	Amp-Hour Reading	Voltage
9:00 a.m.	43.7	−47.5	12.2
9:10 a.m.	25.3	−42.8	13.9
9:20 a.m.	27.5[1]	−38.8	13.9
9:30 a.m.	27.6	−34.1	13.9
10:00 a.m.	22.9	−23.5	13.9
10:30 a.m.	16.0	−14.1	14.0
11:00 a.m.	11.3	−8.2	14.0
11:30 a.m.	7.6	−4.4	14.0
Noon	4.4	−1.6	14.1
12:30 p.m.	3.1	−0.5	14.0
12:47 p.m.	2.4	0.0	14.1

1. During charging the unit frequently cycled and changed the charging rate to a higher value because of the small amp-hour capacity of the battery bank.

needed (the battery bank was 160 amp-hours). This resulted in a rapid increase in the voltage, which caused the switchover to the acceptance stage. In spite of this glitch, the multistage charger did charge faster than the tapered charger, restoring 24 amp-hours in the first hour and 15.3 amp-hours in the second. However, the tapered charger did give a good showing.

We concluded that either of these chargers could put a fast partial charge into your batteries in an hour or so on a cloudy day.

Calculating Charging Time for Multistage Chargers

We recently obtained a formula for calculating the charging time for multistage chargers. It's quite simple:

$$(CAP \times DOD) \div (CC \times 80) = \text{charging time}$$

where CAP = the amp-hour capacity of the battery bank,
DOD = depth of discharge as a percentage,
CC = the maximum charge current of the charger, and
80 = a constant

As an example, let's plug in the test parameters: battery bank capacity is 160 amp-hours, DOD is 25%, and the charger is rated at 40 amps:

$$(160 \times 25) \div (40 \times 80) = 1.25 \text{ hours}$$

Note that this formula does not reflect the elapsed time of Test 2, probably because of the rapid tripping to the second stage. But we think—if used judiciously—the formula can give you a rough estimate of battery recharging time with a multistage charger. If the charger is powered by a generator (see Test 3), the formula will also give you an idea of how long the generator will need to run to do the job.

Test 3: Truecharge 40 Amp Multistage Charger with a Generator

We did another test with the multistage charger, only this time we plugged it into our 1,850-watt portable generator. The generator worked well and did a good job of powering the charger. We measured the amperage output of the generator during start-up and found that it delivered 30 amps momentarily. The batteries were only discharged to a level of −18.5 amp-hours, so it was a short test. After the test began and the initial amperage dropped, we ran a coffeemaker during the charging period with no problems. The batteries were fully charged after 2 hours, 7 minutes.

Table 11-3. Test of Truecharge Multistage Charger (powered by an 1,850-watt Coleman portable generator)		
Time	Charging Amps	Amp-Hour Reading
10:30 a.m.	43.6	−18.5
11:00 a.m.	16.3	−10.7
11:30 a.m.	11.3	−5.4
Noon	6.9	−2.3
12:21 p.m.	5.9	−1.0
12:30 p.m.	4.8	−0.3
12:37 p.m.	4.8	0.0

While we know that −18.5 amp-hours is not a large DOD for a battery, the test still shows how fast a good charger can work even when powered by a portable generator. This generator was able to handle the load of the charger because of its rating of 1,850 watts.

INVERTERS

Inverters produce 120-volt AC power from 12-volt DC batteries, providing the same type of electrical power as a generator. So if you already have a generator, why do you need an inverter? One good reason is convenience. With an inverter, you won't have to start a generator, burn expensive fuel, and create a lot of noise, fumes, or smoke for just a few minutes' use. This is the great advantage of inverters: they can provide power for small purposes quickly and quietly. Inverters are at their best running small loads for short periods of time, while generators are most efficient running big loads for long periods of time.

Inverters are a great addition to any rig for boondocking, providing AC power while dry camping or underway. It is nice to be able to turn on the inverter and use the microwave to heat up a sandwich, brew a cup of coffee, or heat a bowl of soup while stopping at a rest area or along the side of the road. But this level of convenience has a price: you need a large battery bank and the ability to recharge it.

You can also use inverters for battery charging. Many larger inverters (more than 600 watts) have the option of a built-in battery charger. These inverters usually have a multistage or at least a two-stage charger with suitable amperage output for the inverter's size. These chargers work well with a suitably sized generator for providing a rapid recharge.

To understand inverters, we need to explore AC current a bit more. Depending upon how it is generated, AC voltage is expressed as either a sine wave, a square wave, or a modified square wave. As you can see from the illustrations on page 122, a true sine wave is

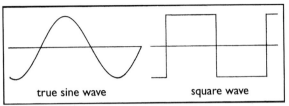

A true sine wave and a square wave.

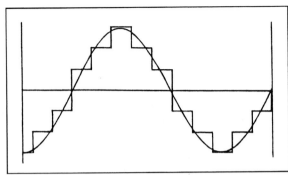

A modified sine wave superimposed over a pure sine wave.

smooth and continuous. It is equivalent to output produced by a generator or an electric company. A square wave is the least efficient form of AC voltage, and a modified square wave is an approximation of a pure sine wave. The electronic switching within an inverter that creates the "steps" of a modified sine wave is really nothing more than the power turning on and off as gets "stepped up" to AC voltage potentials.

Types of Inverters

Square-Wave Inverters

The basic inverter produces voltage in the form of a square wave. Square-wave inverters have been around for years (Bill carried one around Italy in 1958 to run a tape recorder for recording background sounds for a movie he was working on). They are suitable for use with lights, small tools, and resistive loads such as a soldering iron. Usually inexpensive and very heavy, many square-wave inverters do not have any frequency control other than a rheostat knob. The rheostat allows the operator to adjust the voltage, which in turn adjusts the frequency. They are not suitable for use with many electronic appliances such as TVs, VCRs, and microwaves (and it was even risky running a tape recorder with one, as well). These are now obsolete, but we discuss them here for purposes of illustration.

Modified-Sine-Wave Inverters

Modified-sine-wave inverters produce, as mentioned above, a modified sine wave that can power almost all electronic equipment, appliances, and most types of motors. Most good inverters today, from the smallest pocket portable inverters to the largest, permanently mounted units in Class A motorhomes and large trailers, are modified-sine-wave inverters. They are available in sizes from 75 to 2,500 watts and range in price from $25 to several thousand dollars.

Our 600-watt, modified-sine-wave Trace (a company now owned by Xantrex) inverter with its 25 amp tapered charger provided excellent service for eighteen years on two different trailers. The only things we couldn't run on it were a heater, a coffeemaker, a 450-watt

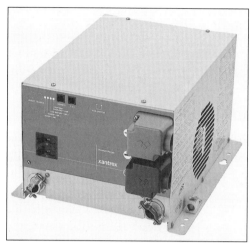

The Xantrex Freedom 458 modified-sine-wave inverter has a built-in 100 amp multistage charger. (Xantrex)

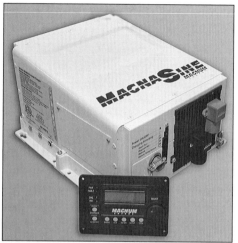

One of the MS Series pure-sine-wave inverter/chargers from Magnum Energy. (Magnum Energy)

microwave (unless it was only for a couple of minutes), and, of course, the air conditioner. We did run our computers, printers, disk drives, color TV, satellite receiver, VCP, and a variety of tools, and never had a problem. We recently acquired a 1,000-watt inverter so we will be able to run things we couldn't before.

Pure-Sine-Wave Inverters

Pure-sine-wave inverters have recently become available for RV use, although most RVers find them too expensive. They can power certain types of equipment that modified-sine-wave inverters can't. They are very expensive and usually only available in larger wattage sizes.

What Size Inverter Should You Buy?

Inverters are rated in wattage, just like generators. They have a surge rating and a continuous or constant rating. The surge rating applies to equipment and appliances that require a high amount of start-up power, such as an electric motor. It is the maximum amount of power the inverter can supply, but only for a short period of time (several seconds to a few minutes). The constant rating is the amount of power the inverter can supply on a steady, ongoing basis to operate appliances and tools.

Choosing the appropriate size for your RV, be it a built-in inverter or a portable one, is quite simple. First determine the total wattage of the items you would most likely power at one time. Then select an inverter that has a constant wattage rating at least 25% higher than the total of these items. This calculation works for all sizes of inverters.

Built-In Battery Chargers

Most inverters over 1,000 watts have a built-in battery charger, usually a multistage charger. You can use this charger instead of the converter/charger supplied in most new RVs, and it will probably do a better job of charging your house battery bank. You can also use the main converter/charger as backup equipment.

Relays and Transfer Switches

Most good-quality inverters—usually those more than 1,000 watts—will have a built-in transfer switch. A transfer switch consists mainly of a double-pole, double-throw relay, which is an electromagnetic solenoid that can handle two circuits. One is the positive wire and the other is the negative one. Think of it as a railroad switch that switches between two tracks, with one rail being the positive circuit and the other, the negative circuit. While a transfer switch can do many things in your electrical system, its primary purpose is to automatically switch the RV's electrical system to campground power from inverter power the moment you plug in. When you unplug from campground power, the relay will automatically switch back to inverter power.

If you have an inverter with a built-in transfer switch, it may be worth the cost of having a good technician wire it for you. It can be very complicated since, by necessity, it must be wired in ahead of the fuse and distribution panel. If your rig has several main circuits and 50 amp service, it could be very involved.

If you have an inverter and 30 amp service that you would like to simply wire in a relay, you can buy just the relay, and if you have the knowledge, do it yourself. You can purchase relays from any Grainger store or online (www.grainger.com). The relay is Dayton model #5X847 and the dust cover is #4A079.

When installing a relay, you must make the field connection on the incoming positive wire from the land-power cable. This is so the main circuit will open to provide the RV park's electricity. When the cable is unplugged, the relay trips back to the inverter side for its service. You must use stranded three-wire cable, so the system will have a grounding green wire. We recommend using triplex boat cable that meets Coast Guard specifications, which has a higher ampacity than any wire used in your RV. Do not use Romex cable in your RV—it is brittle and can break, which can cause a short.

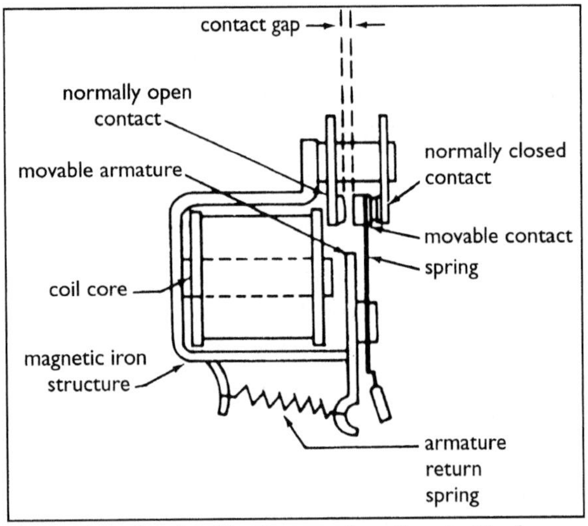

A single-pole, double-throw relay. One half of a double-pole relay is shown. (Dayton Electric Manufacturing Co.)

Small Portable Inverters

Many good, inexpensive portable inverters in the 300- to 1,000- watt range can provide enough wattage to run a small color TV, a radio, or even a computer. Most of these portable inverters have a cord with a cigarette lighter plug on the end so you can plug it into a lighter socket.

We know many RVers who use small pocket inverters, only 150 to 300 watts, to power TVs with satellite dishes and computers with printers. All these pocket or notebook inverters also have a cigarette lighter plug so you can plug it in anywhere you have a lighter socket. They really deliver a lot of power for their size and are easily stored.

However, we really don't hold cigarette lighter sockets in high regard. Manufacturers first made use of them many years ago when some 12-volt appliances, such as

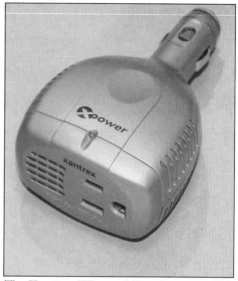

The Xantrex XPower Micro Inverter 175 produces 140 watts of continuous AC power and will run a laptop computer with an attached printer.

small coffeemakers, came on the market for use in your automobile. Manufacturers needed some place to plug them in, and the only available source was the cigarette lighter socket, which we think is a very poor choice.

Our dislike is based on experience. In the 1970s, we owned a small, black-and-white, 12-volt DC TV. It had a strong spring on the center contact of the plug that would pop out of the lighter socket all by itself, disconnecting the TV right when we wanted to watch something.

To their credit, many of today's manufacturers have put an adjustment on the plug that increases the side pressure of the negative contacts on the plug against the walls of the socket.

However, we recently purchased a 140-watt inverter to use for running our computer, and after plugging it into the cigarette lighter socket, we couldn't pull the plug back out. Since we were boondocking at the time, we couldn't leave the inverter plugged in when we were not using it because it ran a small built-in cooling fan, which then became a phantom load. Fortunately, one final, strong pull separated the inverter from the socket.

One of the nice features of these small inverter units is that you select only the appliance you wish to use, no more or less. Whereas if you have a large inverter wired into the RV's AC system, other electrical phantom loads may be inadvertently turned on at the same time you are running your smaller load (see Chapter 8), which can account for a lot of wasted amp-hours of battery capacity.

When we hooked up our new 1,000-watt inverter, we found we were drawing 3 to 4 amps of various phantom loads over and above the loads we were trying to run. The refrigerator was probably part of this, since it drew almost 1 amp of power, but finding the rest of them took some detective work, which involved a lot of turning many circuits and appliances on and off until we found the problems.

Our three-way lighter socket, which is mounted under a cabinet, allows us to plug in a small inverter plus two other pieces of 12-volt equipment.

Wiring

When considering purchasing an inverter, or upgrading one, make sure the wiring in your trailer or motorhome is adequate for the job. We recently installed a three-socket unit over our computer table for boondocking use. The unit has 12-gauge twin wires for hooking up to your system. (It was really designed to be mounted under the dashboard of your car).

The wiring you will be fastening it to will probably be only 14-gauge wire, which is common in RV use. The 140-watt inverter can draw 11.66 amps if it is run at full capacity for 1 hour (140 watts ÷ 12 volts = 11.6666 amps). The ampacity of 14-gauge wire is 20 amps, which has a voltage drop per foot of 0.05231 volt at 20 amps. With a run of 40 feet (the total of both the positive and negative wires to the battery), the inverter would deliver only a theoretical 11.4 volts. So you can see why it is necessary to use the heaviest-gauge wire as much as possible over the shortest distance possible.

Inverter Amperage Draw

While we are doing math, let's go over how to determine the amperage draw (in DC amp-hours) of an inverter. The formula is :

$$\text{wattage of the appliance to be used} \div 12 \text{ volts} \times$$
$$1.1 \text{ (an efficiency factor)} \times \text{hours of operation} = \text{amp-hours}$$

For example, if you run a 200-watt appliance for 9.6 minutes, the equation would be:

$$(200 \text{ watts} \div 12) \times 1.1 \times 0.16 \text{ hour} = 2.93 \text{ amp-hours}$$

If you have the appliance's amperage instead of the wattage, then you can use that and not do the voltage division.

If you want to determine amperage draw for an AC appliance, remember that 1 amp of AC equates to 10 amps of DC. So, for example, 5 amps of AC becomes 50 amps of DC when it comes from the batteries via an inverter.

Battery Bank Size

Next let's consider the proper size of the battery bank needed to safely operate a large inverter. There are two ways to calculate this size. Going back to our Rule of Twenty-Fives (Chapter 9), the first rule was never apply a load greater than 25% of amp-hour battery capacity.

Applying this rule, we can calculate the minimum size of a battery bank for an inverter:

inverter wattage ÷ 12 × 4 = minimum battery bank size in amp-hours

Dividing the watts by 12 volts gives the load size; multiplying by 4 gives the 25% capacity of the battery bank in amp-hours. Here's an example:

1,000 watts ÷ 12 × 4 = 333.33 amp-hours

This would be the safest minimal size battery bank to use with this inverter, although we believe it would be prudent to make the bank even larger than the calculated figure. One inverter manufacturer states in its literature that 50% of capacity can be used. The reason is that most inverters operate for only a few minutes at a time, and the batteries will not be damaged with that amount of short-term use. To recalculate our example:

1,500 watts ÷ 12 × 2 = 250 amp-hours

The manufacturer is probably right because you rarely run an inverter at full rating, and so the load would be smaller than required by the full rating. However, we would still be cautious in operating a 1,500-watt inverter with such a small battery bank capacity, and would be more comfortable with a battery bank capacity of 440 amp-hours.

Although there are large inverters capable of operating high-wattage items, such as an air conditioner, these items are very poor loads because of their high-current demand.

SYSTEM SIZE

The capacity of your battery bank and your charging equipment should be something that suits your individual needs. If you don't use an air conditioner while boondocking, you may not need a large generator. If you don't want to run a microwave, a small-wattage inverter may be satisfactory.

Remember that with any equipment, the higher the wattage output, the more it will cost. You can start out with a very modest charging system and then upgrade it gradually, if necessary, according to your needs. Our original setup included the following:

- ■ 160 amp-hour battery bank
- ■ 600-watt inverter/charger
- ■ two 40-watt solar panels and one 48-watt solar panel, totaling 128 watts

This system was adequate for our limited needs in our old trailer as long as we were conservative in our appliance use. However, we later added a 1,850-watt portable generator to take care of battery charging on cloudy days when the solar panels were not working at peak efficiency.

Using the tables we've provided, you can calculate your own typical amp-hour and wattage consumption, and then design your system accordingly. If you do a lot of boondocking, it's a good idea to have at least two means of battery charging.

A FEW WORDS OF CAUTION

Finally, we offer a couple of thoughts about generator and inverter safety. Many of these units are wired with the ground (safety) conductor and the neutral conductor bonded together, which can be a very unsafe condition in an RV. This configuration grounds the metal of the RV's skin to a current-carrying conductor, thus creating the possibility of an electrical shock if you touch the side of the RV. To be on the safe side, have a knowledgeable electrician check your equipment for you to see if yours has this type of wiring. Our 1,850-watt portable Coleman generator had a sticker on it stating that the generator had a "floating neutral" (not bonded to the RV chassis), which meant it was safe to use.

Fuses

Installing a fuse in the positive wire from the inverter to the battery is a necessary safety precaution. But you must use a fuse designated for DC use. Using an AC fuse is dangerous since if the fuse blows, the current can fuse or arc across the gap in the fuse. Use a Class-T DC fuse in a proper insulated fuse holder designed to prevent accidental contact with the fuse or the studs. Select a fuse size that is at least 25% larger than the maximum load the fuse is designed to protect. We have a 100 amp fuse on our 600-watt inverter positive lead, for instance. It is also a good idea to install a 300 amp fuse on the main ground wire of the batteries where it connects to the chassis ground and the ground side of the circuit breaker panel bus. This will act as a catastrophe fuse in the event of a major electrical short or failure, preventing your RV from burning to the ground.

Ground Fault Circuit Interrupters

Most small to medium-sized inverters have a ground fault circuit interrupter (GFCI) installed in the receptable. If you have a transfer switch (relay) in your AC wiring between the land-power cable and either an inverter or generator, you may find that the GFCI will constantly trip whenever you try to use the inverter. It may be necessary to change the receptacle to one without a GFCI to get the equipment to work.

CHAPTER 12

Sun and Wind Power

We think all serious boondock campers should consider using solar power and wind power. When you're "off the grid," it's great to be able to keep your batteries charged with alternative energy sources. We have had a lot of experience with solar panels over the years. In 1989 we bought two 40-watt panels producing 2.55 amps each when we acquired our first 29-foot fifth-wheel trailer. They did a good job for us in a limited way. A few years later we added a used 48-watt, 3.02 amp panel, and this increased our maximum charging capability to a total of 8.12 amps. When we traded the old trailer for a new 34-foot fifth-wheel just four years ago, we replaced all our old panels with two new 85-watt panels producing 4.72 amps each, plus a 100-watt, 4.51 amp panel. The 100-watt panel has a lower operating amperage than the 85-watt panels do, but it has a much higher operating voltage of 21.5 volts

(RVIA)

instead of the 18 volts of the 85-watt panels. We now have more than an ample charging capability of 13.9 amps for all of our boondocking needs, and at times the amperage has been even higher, which we will explain later.

Solar panels have become more and more popular with RVers, and many RVs are manufactured with installed solar panels. Wind generators haven't gotten as much publicity, but we're familiar with them because we lived aboard a sailboat for twelve years.

SOLAR POWER

Solar power is probably the most popular and best way to charge your batteries and offers many benefits to RVers:

- Quiet: there are no moving parts to create noise.

- Clean: there is no fuel or oil to clean up.

- Safe: since there is no combustible fuel, there are no risks of fires or carbon monoxide poisoning; the low levels of electricity generated means there is a reduced risk of shocks

- Easy: there is no maintenance except keeping dust off the panels; there are no complicated start-up steps—you just turn on the controller.

- Efficient: it takes the free energy from the sun and turns it into pure DC electricity.

- Good for your batteries: since it generates pure DC current, it charges your batteries slowly and steadily.

Solar panels give RVers more independence when boondocking.(AM Solar)

SELECTING A SOLAR POWER SYSTEM

A solar power system consists of the panels, a controller, the batteries, and an inverter. We've covered batteries and inverters elsewhere; here we'll focus on the first two components.

What's important when you go looking for a solar power system? Here are some things to keep in mind:

- First and foremost, make sure the panels are rated for RV use. Many bargain systems are not.

- Have a good idea of what your daily amp-hour consumption will be so you can talk knowledgeably with the dealer.

- Look at the specifications: watt rating, amps delivered, tolerance, peak power voltage (see the Solar Panels section).

- Know your budget. The cost of a basic charging system with one panel rated at 50 watts should be around $395. This should include the panel, the controller, the mounting brackets, and the necessary wiring, but not an inverter. More elaborate four-panel systems can run to as much as $4,000 to $5,000 for everything you'll need. Individual panel prices can run from $295 to $700 depending on wattage size without a controller or the wiring. Controllers and regulators range in price from $45 to $350.

- Make sure you have the right components for your proposed system. Is everything you need there and functioning?

SOLAR PANELS

Solar panels are made up of photovoltaic (PV) cells, which basically means they create electricity from light. The basic unit of a panel is a cell. Cells are wired together to form a module, or panel, and panels are wired together to form an array. There are 30 to 36 cells per panel, each generating about 0.5 volt. The voltage of a cell remains constant, but the number of cells and the total area they cover determines amperage.

Cells are made from silicon, which is derived from quartz. The high-grade quartz

Buyer Beware: How Much Will It Cost?

Be on the lookout for misleading information. If you look through the magazine ads or go on the Internet, you'll find many companies offering solar packages that promise you can have so many hours of power for your electrical needs. But often they are offering panels and equipment not suited for RV use.

Some ads express these figures in watts per day, which are not useful ratings, as they usually are not achieved. Other ads state that a package will give you AC power for your TV, computer, and other appliances, when all a solar system will give you is DC power for battery charging. If you want to run AC appliances off your batteries, make sure—*before you buy*—that the solar power system package includes a suitable inverter to convert 12 VDC battery power to 120 VAC.

So as you shop for a solar power system, be an informed consumer. The information in this chapter will give you a good start.

used for the cells is mined and then refined to produce nearly pure silicon. Crystalline silicon is grown in the form of large crystals, which are cut into thin wafers to form cells. These cells can take one of three forms:

1. Monocrystalline cells are single-crystal cells that produce 0.5 volt and are the most efficient.

2. Polycrystalline cells have many crystal pieces per cell. They are cheaper to produce than single-crystal cells, but also less efficient.

3. Amorphous cells are thin-film cells with no crystalline structure. They are made by depositing vaporized silicon onto a metal substrate. They are the least expensive to produce, and also the least efficient.

Choosing Solar Panels

Solar panels are rated in watts, which are derived by multiplying the panel's peak power voltage by its peak power amperage (remember, watts = volts × amps). These ratings are based on standard test conditions of 1,000 watts per square meter of light input, a cell temperature of 77°F, and an air mass of 1.5 (slightly above sea level). These conditions are rarely found in real-world operation, but manufacturers had to settle on standard parameters so that panels could be rated after being subjected to the same test conditions. This gives buyers a basis for comparing panels from various manufacturers.

As a boondocker, it is important to know the peak power voltage of your panels because efficiency decreases as cell temperature increases. We learned this the hard way one year at Quartzsite on a moderately warm January day. The panels were in full sunlight and they got so hot because of their dark color that the voltage dropped to the point that we were getting only couple of amps of charge into the batteries. These older panels had a maximum peak power voltage of only 15.7 volts, so a 2-volt drop greatly affected the charging rate. We decided that if this happened again, we would try to restore full power by pouring cold water over the panels to cool them. However, before we got the chance, we purchased new panels. These had a peak power voltage of over 17 volts—a much better rating.

Table 12-1 lists specific brands of solar panels along with their specifications.

Another important specification to check is the manufacturing tolerance used in producing the panels. Most manufacturers use a 10% tolerance, which means that your 100-watt panel may, in actuality, only produce 90 watts. Look for companies that use a higher tolerance, perhaps 5%, since this means the panel's output should be closer to its rated wattage.

How many solar panels do you need to boondock? It depends on the type of panels and their intended use. We'll look at a few ways to answer this question:

■ Use 1 watt of solar panel output for every 2 amp-hours (1:2) of battery capacity—for example, a 50-watt panel with a 100 amp-hour battery. This is only a rough guide, but in our experience we have found that one 48-watt

Table 12-1. Solar Panel Specifications						
Manufacturer[1]	Model Number	Wattage	Rated Peak Power (volts)	Rated Peak Power (amps)	Number of Cells	Size (in.)
AM Solar	AM65	65	17.6	3.7	36	59.25 x 14.0
	AM100	100	21.5	4.54	44	57.25 x 21.25
BP Solar	BP380	80	17.6	4.55	36	47.6 x 21.1
	BP3125	125	17.6	7.1	36	59.4 x 26.5
Evergreen	EC-115-GD	115	17.2	6.65	72	62.5 x 25.69
GE	GEPV-100	100	16.1	6.2	36	58.1 x 26.0
Kyocera	KC80	80	16.9	4.73	36	38.4 x 25.7
	KC125	125	17.4	7.12	36	58.0 x 26.0
Matrix	PW750	90	17.8	5.0	36	48.7 x 21.9
Sharp	SP60	60	17.0	3.31	36	38.5 x 17.5
	ND-L3E6E	123	17.2	7.16	36	59.0 x 26.0
Shell Solar	SQ80-P	80	16.9	4.76	36	47.2 x 20.8

1. Because of the great demand for solar products, the listed panels may be altered, changed, or discontinued by the manufacturers and may not be available.

panel will, in bright sunshine, easily charge a 105 amp-hour battery with a modest DOD of 10% to 20% of capacity. If you have two 6-volt golf-cart batteries of 220 amp-hours, you would probably need about 110 watts of panel power, or two 53-watt panels (although two 48-watt panels would suffice with diminished electrical use).

■ If you spend a lot of time in the Northwest, as we do, use a more conservative guide: 1.5 watts of panel output per 2 amp-hours (1.5:2). For example, use a 75-watt panel with a 100 amp-hour battery.

■ Use your daily consumption estimate from Chapter 8. For a daily use of 30 amp-hours, you'd need two panels capable of delivering 15 amp-hours per day.

■ Identify when you'll do most of your boondocking—summer or winter. If in summer, figure on getting about 40 amp-hours of charging time per day, and in the winter, about 30 amp-hours (with full sunshine). Then factor in your need to return 1.2 amps to the batteries per 1.0 amp used. As an example, if you have one 100-watt panel, your daily use could be 33 amp-hours per day in the summer (33 Ah × 1.2 = 39.6 Ah) and 25 amp-hours in the winter (25 Ah × 1.2 = 30 Ah).

Keep in mind that these estimates are for minimal charging capabilities. You honestly can never have too many solar panels. It would be nice to have an array delivering up to 30 amps of charging power, and it is now possible. Only your budget and your RV's roof size define the limits. Our current solar system provides 1.28 watts of panel per 1 amp-hour of battery capacity, which gives us a large amount of backup charging capability. The main thing is that a minimal number of panels can do the job, if you control and limit the amount of battery discharge.

Also, other factors may affect the actual charge rates of your panels, so they may occasionally deliver much more than the estimates suggest, such as a boost when cloud conditions permit it.

Remember Rule 7 from Chapter 9: "Never discharge your batteries to more than your charging equipment's capability to recharge them within the next daily charge period." We can see here that this rule definitely applies to the use of solar panels.

Insolation

Insolation is a measure (in kilowatt-hours per square meter—kWh/m^2) of equivalent full sun-hours. A sun-hour is the maximum, or 100%, of sunlight shining on a module for 1 full hour. Even though the sun may shine for 14 hours from sunrise to sunset, the same light intensity is not falling on your panels constantly. The amount of insolation received varies according to the angle of the sun (which varies daily and seasonally), the state of the atmosphere, the altitude, and geographic location.

When the sun rises in the morning, the flat angle of the sun's rays causes a lower output because of the reflection of light off the surface of the panels and the density of the atmosphere. Only the sunlight at noon penetrates the thinnest portion of the atmosphere and therefore gives maximum amperage output. As the sun sets, the rays again have to penetrate more of the atmosphere so the amperage starts to drop. In general, the hours from 9 a.m. to 3 p.m. are the best hours of sunshine during both the winter and summer. So it is important to calculate or monitor your amp-hour battery consumption every night. (For more on solar panel output, see the Solar Panel Tests section later in the chapter, which includes hourly solar output tables.)

Maps and tables showing insolation values are available for people building or equipping homes for solar operation. They are less useful for RVers, since we are usually traveling from one part of the country to another. But they do show how effective solar panels are in different areas, so we've included an example here. We have developed our own method of estimating panel size based on insolation values as seen in the scenarios below.

Scenario 1: Let's say you only go RVing in the summer, and/or you have minimal battery requirements; you can use 48 amp-hours as your average daily amp-hour usage. Because it's summer, figure 8 hours of usable sunlight (although it won't always be at full intensity). Divide your daily amp-hour use by the number of hours of sunlight to estimate the solar panel amperage output you'll need. (The extra time the panels will be delivering amperage will make up for the fact that they will probably not be at their rated amperage for the full 8 hours.)

$$48 \text{ amp-hours} \div 8 \text{ hours} = 6 \text{ amps}$$

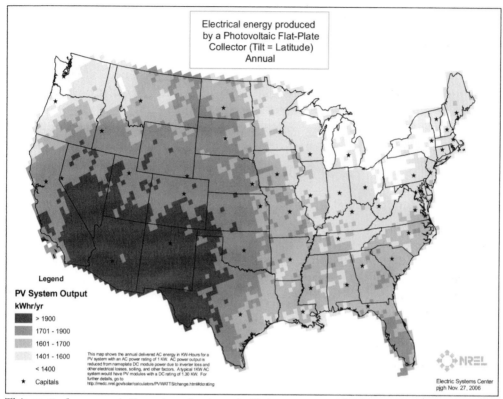

This map shows variations in solar panel efficiency across the United States. (Renewable Resource Data Center, National Renewable Energy Laboratory)

In this example, an array of two 48-watt, 3 amp panels might be sufficient for most of your needs.

Scenario 2: You are a snowbird or a fulltimer and go south every winter; let's use 65 amp-hours as your average daily amp-hour usage and 6 hours of usable sunlight:

$$65 \text{ amp-hours} \div 6 \text{ hours} = 10.3 \text{ amps}$$

In this case, you should have a minimum of two 90- or 100-watt panels of 5 amps each.

Scenario 3: Let's work this problem backward using 6 hours of usable sunlight and the amperage output of the panels we currently use, 13.9, to calculate how much we can discharge our batteries:

$$6 \text{ hours} \times 13.9 \text{ amps} = 83.4 \text{ amp-hours}$$

This tells us we could discharge our batteries a total of 83.4 amp-hours, or approximately 40% of our batteries' capacity, and still recharge the batteries during the next day's charging period. But we would need a good amount of full sunlight during this period with no shadows on the panels.

Scenario 4: You plan to travel to Alaska or the Pacific Northwest, where insolation decreases. Your average daily amp-hour usage is 60 amp-hours, and let's use 4 hours of usable sunlight:

$$60 \text{ amp-hours} \div 4 \text{ hours} = 15 \text{ amps}$$

Here two 120-watt, 7.5 amp panels would most likely do the job for you.

SOLAR PANEL TESTS

We conducted three separate tests with our solar panels: two tests to determine the efficiency of our solar panels, and the third test to check their battery-charging capabilities.

Test 1: Solar Efficiency

The object of this test was to determine the actual maximum amperage that our solar panels were capable of delivering on a bright, sunny day.

Conditions

Our solar panel array consisted of two 40-watt panels and one 48-watt panel, which had a combined total of 8.12 amps maximum output. The panels were installed on the sloped roof of our fifth-wheel trailer.

We ran the first test at a park near Carlsbad, New Mexico, on March 10, 1998. Since this is about the halfway point between the winter solstice and the summer solstice, we thought this time of year and location would give us an accurate average output of our panel array. The sun rose at 6:22 a.m. Mountain Time and set at 6:10 p.m., for a total of almost 12 hours of sunlight.

We started our test at 7:00 a.m. and ended at 5 p.m.—10 hours of charging time. For this test, we didn't charge our batteries. Instead, we turned on several lights to create a good load and force the panels to deliver their full amperage.

Results

Table 12-2 and the graph show the output we recorded each hour throughout the day. In spite of the small amount of charging per hour, the total of 47.1 amp-hours

Table 12-2. Solar Panel Output for a Typical Day	
Time	Output (amps)
7:00 a.m.	0.4
8:00 a.m.	1.6
9:00 a.m.	3.4
10:00 a.m.	5.1
11:00 a.m.	6.2
Noon	6.7
1:00 p.m.	6.9
2:00 p.m.	6.4
3:00 p.m.	5.3
4:00 p.m.	3.7
5:00 p.m.	1.8
	Total: 47.1

was impressive, translating to an average hourly output of 4.71 amps and an efficiency of 58%.

You may notice, either from the table or the graph, that the panels never produced their maximum output. There is a reason for this. Although the panels were mounted on the 15-degree roof slope of our fifth-wheel trailer, the rear of the trailer was pointed to the northwest, so the panels didn't have a good sun angle. As you can see, this cost us 1.2 amps at maximum output. In spite of this, the panels still produced a good output.

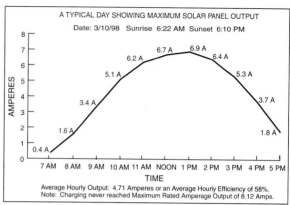

A graph of the typical solar output of our solar panels.

Test 2: Solar Efficiency

The object of our second test was to further determine the panels' maximum amperage output.

Conditions

We conducted this test a month later in Midland, Texas, this time ensuring that the rear of our trailer pointed to the south so the panels were at the proper angle to the sun. We used the same panels: two 40-watt panels and one 48-watt panel.

The sky was clear with no clouds when we began the test, although a light cloud cover appeared later. The sun rose at 7:02 a.m. Central Time and set at 7:56 p.m., for a total of almost 13 hours of sunlight. We began recording readings at 8 a.m. and ended at 7 p.m., for a total of 11 hours of testing time.

Results

During this test, our amperage output total was 71.2 amp-hours, with an hourly average of 5.93 amps and a 73% efficiency. Between noon and 3 p.m. our panels delivered over their maximum rated amperage output of 8.12 amps. This happens when there is a light cloud cover but the sun still shines through brightly. The sunlight bounces between the ground and the clouds, which can increase the intensity of the sunlight.

Table 12-3. Maximum Solar Panel Output for a Typical Day

Time	Output (amps)
8:00 a.m.	0.5
9:00 a.m.	2.6
10:00 a.m.	5.1
11:00 a.m.	7.2
Noon	8.4
1:00 p.m.	9.3[1]
2:00 p.m.	9.3[1]
3:00 p.m.	8.9
4:00 p.m.	7.8
5:00 p.m.	6.3
6:00 p.m.	4.0
7:00 p.m.	1.8
	Total: 71.2

1. The panels produced a maximum of 9.3 amps for over 2 hours, which is higher than the 8.12 amp rated output.

The results of these two tests show the high efficiency of solar panels, and their capability to recharge batteries quickly during the charge period if you monitor discharges to match the solar output.

Test 3: Charging Batteries

On June 28, 1998, while in Albany, Oregon, we ran a test to determine the charging capability of our solar panels.

Conditions

We were still using the same solar panels, two 40-watt panels and one 48-watt panel, with a maximum amperage output of 8.12 amps and a total wattage rating of 128 volts. We also used an early shunt-diode regulator.

Our batteries were discharged to −48.9 amp-hours according to the amp-hour meter. The trailer was oriented west-northwest so the panels were pointing more or less toward the morning sun. Sunrise was at 5:24 a.m. Pacific Time and sunset was at 6:10 p.m. The sky was clear with bright sun and no clouds came up during the day.

We turned on the solar panels at 8 a.m. and recorded until 5:50 p.m., when the batteries were completely charged. The total time was 9 hours and 50 minutes. This may seem like a long time, but the batteries were discharged to 30% of capacity, and we were in Oregon, a poor area for maximum sunlight because of the low angle of the sun.

Results

Our average hourly output for this test was 6.27 amps, with an average hourly efficiency of 77.2%. It was interesting that during the peak hours of charging from 10 a.m. to 2:30 p.m., the charging amps ranged between 7.1 and 8.1 amps, close to the maximum panel output. Consequently, 27 amp-hours (55% of total charging) were restored to the batteries during this period.

There were two items of interest during this test. First, there was a slight drop in amperage at 12:30 p.m. As there was no apparent change in the sunlight at the time, we believe this was due to the panels getting too hot, which can cause voltage drop. A good breeze came up shortly thereafter, which cooled the panels and restored the efficiency. The second item was the drop in charging that occurred at 4 p.m., when without thinking someone turned on four interior cabin lights. Note the large drops in charging (1.2 amps per light) and voltage because of the load.

We think this test stretched the limits of charging with the panels we were using then and the large discharge of 30%. It would have been better for us to limit our DOD to around 20%.

SOLAR CONTROLLERS

A controller, or regulator, controls the amount of voltage produced by the panels and holds it to the proper level to effectively and efficiently charge the batteries. The controller also

Table 12-4. Charging Test with Three Solar Panels			
Time	Charging Amps	Amp-Hour Reading	Battery Voltage
8:00 a.m.	4.0	−48.9	12.1
8:30 a.m.	5.2	−46.8	13.0
9:00 a.m.	5.9	−44.8	13.2
9:30 a.m.	6.5	−42.8	13.2
10:00 a.m.	7.1	−39.5	13.2
10:30 a.m.	7.5	−36.8	13.2
11:00 a.m.	7.7	−33.8	13.3
11:30 a.m.	8.0	−30.9	13.3
Noon	8.1	−27.5	13.3
12:30 p.m.	7.9[1]	−24.8	13.2
1:00 p.m.	8.1	−21.6	13.3
1:30 p.m.	7.7	−18.2	13.4
2:00 p.m.	7.5	−15.5	13.4
2:30 p.m.	7.2	−12.3	13.4
3:00 p.m.	6.9	−8.6	13.5
3:30 p.m.	6.5	−6.7	13.5
4:00 p.m.	5.8	−6.4[2]	13.4
4:30 p.m.	5.0	−4.6	13.7
5:00 p.m.	3.9	−3.0	13.7
5:30 p.m.	2.9	−1.8	13.7
5:50 p.m.	2.4	00.0	13.6

1. No explainable reason for drop in output unless the panels overheated (see text).
2. This drop occurred because four lights (1.2 amps each) were inadvertently turned on for 30 minutes.

prevents a reverse flow of current at night when the panels are not producing (otherwise, the batteries would discharge as the current flowed back into the panels). There are two basic types of controllers—series-pass controllers and shunt-type controllers—and they come in a variety of amperage outputs, ranging from several amps to 40 amps.

Series-Pass Controllers

A series-pass controller is wired into the charge circuit, on either the positive or negative lead, in series with the battery. It turns off current flow when the voltage reaches a certain set value, when the batteries are charged. When the batteries are discharged, and the voltage drops to yet another set voltage value, the controller turns the current back on. Usually a series-pass controller contains a relay, which switches the current flow off and on. Some series-pass controllers use MOSFETs (metal oxide semiconductor field effect transistors) or SCRs (silicon-controlled rectifiers) instead of a relay to switch circuits on and off in response to a control signal.

Shunt Controllers

A shunt controller is a solid-state device installed across the positive and negative leads from the panels. It diverts the current flow back to the panels once the set voltage is reached and the batteries are charged. In effect, a shunt controller works by short-circuiting the panels. Shunt controllers also employ a diode in the positive lead to prevent reverse current flow at night and when other charging devices are used (e.g., an engine alternator, converter/charger, or portable charger).

Selecting a Controller

When selecting a controller, look for one with a high enough amperage output to handle (1) your present needs, (2) any future additions to your panel array, and (3) those times when your panels may deliver more than their rated output. A good rule of thumb in choosing a controller is that the controller should be able to handle current at least 25% higher than the panel array amperage output.

Although there are two basic types of controllers, you have several options to choose from.

Multistage Charging

Multistage charging is available with both series-pass and shunt controllers. It uses the same charging stages we've become familiar with: bulk stage, absorption stage, float stage, and equalization stage. Not all controllers utilize all four stages, and some offer the equalizing stage as automatic or manual, or both.

Pulse-Width Modulation

A technology available in many regular and multistage controllers is pulse-width modulation (PWM). PWM maintains the full flow of current (instead of tapering off as the battery becomes charged), but it varies the length of time the full current is applied using pulses. These pulses are created by switching the current on and off, and varying the lengths of time, from longer On periods to longer Off ones. Switching and pulsing occurs very rapidly, usually in microseconds. The advantage is the batteries have a higher charge acceptance rate with pulse charging because each pulse is at the highest current rate the panels can provide. With PWM, the current from a solar array varies according to the battery's condition and recharging needs.

Two-Stage Charging

Several controllers now offer two-stage charging with a bulk stage and an absorption stage for the best possible method to charge your batteries.

MPPT

A few controllers have incorporated a new technology called maximum power point tracking (MPPT). MPPT converts excessive voltage available from solar panels into additional current for battery charging. This current "boost" can be 30% or more.

MPPT technology is similar in purpose to an automatic car transmission, which shifts to keep the engine at the best rpm. During the day, as lighting conditions change and affect the maximum power available, the MPPT controller adjusts many times a minute to keep the charging rate at the highest amperage output possible. In other words, it is tracking the maximum power point, thus the term MPPT. These current increases are highly variable, and depend on the intensity of the light, the panel temperature, and the discharge level of the voltage of the batteries. The colder the panel temperature and the greater the difference between the panel voltage and the battery voltage, the greater the boost, or gain, will be of the charging amperage. The current increases tend to be greatest in cooler conditions when days are short, the sun is low on the horizon, and batteries may be more highly discharged.

To illustrate how this feature works, we'll use a 75-watt panel with a rated peak power voltage of 17 volts and a peak power amperage of 4.4 amps. The batteries have been discharged to 12.2 volts, a DOD of about 50%. Because of the difference between the rated output voltage of the panel and the battery voltage, 21.12 watts are, in effect, being wasted:

$$17 \text{ volts (peak power)} - 12.2 \text{ volts discharged} = 4.8 \text{ volts}$$

$$4.8 \text{ volts} \times 4.4 \text{ amps (peak power)} = 21.12 \text{ watts}$$

We did a lot of our early tests with MPPT on the Solar-Boost 2000E, made by Blue Sky Energy (www.blueskyenergyinc.com), which is a very good controller. It has a multistage PWM charging system, and was one of the first to have this sophisticated means of control. Most recently, we tested a new controller, the Heliotrope HPV-22B (www.heliotrope-pv.com). It is also a very good controller, and we are still using it.

Both controllers have LCD panel readouts that show charging voltage, the amperage coming from the panel array, and the total boosted amperage. The Heliotrope controller also has a three-stage (PWM) charging system with bulk, absorption, and float stages. It is also designed to work with a converter/charger when plugged into shore power. Both controllers offer temperature sensors that control the charge voltage.

The HPV-22B has two new features that improve on its predecessor, the HPV-220: an On/Off switch and a Dry Camp/Shore Power switch. The On/Off switch means you don't need to install a separate switch in the positive lead from the panels to turn them on or off. There are times when you don't want the panels to operate, especially when you want to rest your fully charged batteries after a recent charge.

The Dry Camp/Shore Power switch lets you engage or disengage the float mode. When set to the Dry Camp position, the controller charge set point is 14.3 to 14.4 volts to allow full charging of the batteries from the panels. When in the Shore Power position, the float mode is engaged and holds the voltage at 13.2 volts. If a small load (or loads) comes online, the controller allows the required amperage to flow, as long as the float voltage can be maintained. The important thing is that heavier loads can sometimes trip most controllers to return to the high bulk stage voltage. If after being fully charged the batteries are subjected to 14.4 voltage for long, they can be overcharged, causing the plates to dry out.

We installed an HPV-22B in our rig for testing. It controls our two 85-watt and one 100-watt panels. Recently while driving down I-5, and with fully charged batteries, we left the switch set to Shore Power. Periodic monitoring showed that the controller was

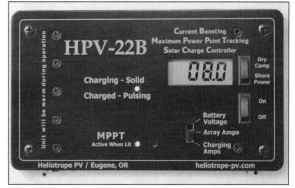

The Heliotrope HPV-22B solar panel controller.
(Heliotrope)

Table 12-5. Heliotrope HPV-30 Evaluation[1]

Time	Xantrex Link 10			HPV-30 Solar Monitor				Daystar Meter	Scientific Weather Remote		Boost Amps	% Boost
	Amp-Hour Reading	Battery Voltage	Amps	Battery Voltage	Array Amps	Charging Amps	Stage	Insolation[2]	Outside Temperature (°F)	Humidity (%)		
8:30 a.m.	−29.4	12.7	0.3	12.7	0.4	0.2	bulk	028 W/m²	53.2	74	0	0
9:30 a.m.	−27.2	13.05	4.8	13.0	2.8	4.8	bulk	275 W/m²	61.0	65	2.0	71.4[3]
10:00 a.m.[2]	−24.7	13.2	5.9	12.2	4.1	5.8	bulk	355 W/m²	64.9	56	1.7	46.4
10:30 a.m.	−22.1	13.3	6.7	13.3	4.8	6.7	bulk	422 W/m²	69.4	54	1.9	39.5
11:00 a.m.	−18.4	13.4	7.5	13.4	5.5	7.4	bulk	498 W/m²	67.8	57	1.9	34.5
11:30 a.m.	−15.1	13.6	8.1	13.6	6.0	8.0	bulk	571 W/m²	69.1	54	2.0	33.3
Noon	−12.0	13.9	8.2	13.9	6.0	8.0	bulk	630 W/m²	71.2	50	2.0	33.3
12:20 p.m.	−12.0	13.9	8.2	14.2	6.2	7.8	bulk	630 W/m²	71.2	50	2.0	33.3
12:23 p.m.	−9.1	14.4	7.3	14.4	5.6	7.6	taper	625 W/m²	73.0	44	2.0	35.7
12:45 p.m.	−6.9	14.4	5.2	14.4	3.6	5.2	taper	630 W/m²	73.2	39	1.6	44.4
1:15 p.m.	−5.1	14.4	3.8	14.4	2.6	3.9	taper	645 W/m²	73.9	37	1.3	50.0
1:31 p.m.	−4.4	13.1	0.1	13.4	0.3	0.0	float	630 W/m²	73.9	34	0	0

1. Date of test: 9/20/05; Location: Springfield, Oregon.
2. Insolation readings based on 1,000 watts per square meter.
3. We changed the interval between readings so that we could determine the exact time of changeover from bulk to absorption and from absorption to float.

holding the batteries to a constant 13.2 volts with no amperage output. Yet when we turned on several lights and the water pump, the controller delivered the amps necessary to handle the loads. Pretty good for a solar panel controller.

While we were testing the HPV-22B, we also tested Heliotrope's new HPV-30. This controller can handle panels up to a total of 30 amps, and in a motorhome, can also charge the engine battery (the SLI battery) as well as the house batteries.

During the tests we experienced a remarkable MPPT boost of 71.4%. We attributed this large increase to the 100-watt panel's high peak power voltage of 21.5 volts and the atmospheric conditions that morning.

Our Experience

We used a shunt controller during the early years and were reasonably happy with it. However, after we installed an amp-hour meter, we discovered the panels would not charge the batteries fully enough to "zero" the meter (see Chapter 9). The problem was that when the battery voltage reached the upper set limit, the panels shut off until the battery voltage had dropped to the lowest set voltage. The charging process wasn't held at the set-point voltage long enough to completely charge the batteries, and the amperage wasn't allowed to taper off. The result was that the batteries were only getting about 75% of their total charge. We eventually solved the problem with a multistage controller.

INSTALLING YOUR SOLAR POWER SYSTEM

Properly installing your solar power system takes careful thought and planning. Before you climb on the roof, solar panel in hand, you'll need to make some decisions.

Placement and Orientation

How and where do you want to place the solar panels on the roof? If you are only installing a two-panel system, the answer is fairly easy, but if you are planning on four, six, or even more panels, then it takes more planning. You have limited space, and there are other things on the roof to take into consideration. Do you have a satellite dish, for example, or an air conditioner or swamp cooler? Shadows from any of these items will affect solar panel performance. Once during a test, Bill left a pen lying on the panel while he was taking readings. Removing the pen from the panel caused an almost 2 amp jump in output. One of the most important points is not locating panels too close to other structures on the roof.

You also have to decide whether your panels should go across the width of the RV or along its length. On our first panel-equipped RV, we installed the panels lengthwise because the roof had a 15-degree angle as it rose from the rear to the front. (It was a fifth-wheel trailer, and the slope provided the necessary headroom in the bedroom). So the roof of the front area was higher than the roof along the rest of the trailer; in effect, the roof had a permanent tilt. When camping, we always tried to find a site that ran north and south so we could back the trailer in facing south.

Tilt

Should you tilt your panels and follow the sun? In the winter it might be a good idea to elevate one side of the panels between 15 to 25 degrees so they face toward the south. This orientation will make your panels more efficient, but we don't see the need in the summer. We have seen rigs with their panels mounted on racks that allow them to swing around to track the sun. Frankly, this just seems like too much work to us, plus we don't really think it's necessary. Also, when panels are tilted up, they can be more easily damaged by the high winds that occur during the winter months, particularly in desert areas.

Three 100-watt solar panels installed lengthwise on the roof of a friend's motorhome.

A problem we experienced in Alaska is that solar panels there do not deliver their full power at any time if they are mounted flat on the roof. Although the summer sun shines for many hours, in some areas as many as 20 hours a day, it is very low in the sky most of the time, similar to the early and late hours of the day in the lower forty-eight states. Tilting and tracking the panels will help a lot, although the amps delivered are still reduced because of the dense atmosphere. If you tilt your panels, you can adjust them for your latitude to make them more efficient, which is good for long-term stays.

Tilting your panels allows you to raise panels perpendicularly to catch more of the sun's rays in the winter or when the sun is low on the horizon in the summer, such as in Alaska. If this is the way you want to go, then place your panels fore and aft. You can use a tilt bar (a length of angled aluminum with bolt holes in each end) to lift them.

Wiring

The next stage is figuring the wire run. Professional installers tell me this is the hardest part of the job because of the work involved.

There are three places you can route the wire through the roof without making a hole: the two vent pipes for the holding tanks and the refrigerator vent. Your choice will be dictated by the proximity of the vents to the battery location. The holding tank vents are usually in one of the interior walls of the RV, which are hollow. The walls of the bathroom, shower room, or toilet room are likely choices for running wires. These walls can also be good places to locate the charge controller and any other instruments you wish to install.

The refrigerator roof vent is another option, but only if it is not located in a slideout. Otherwise, the wiring must be connected to springs or arranged so that it would not be caught or damaged as the slide moves in and out.

Table 12-6. Solar Panel Adjustment by Latitude		
Latitude (degrees)[1]	Angle of Tilt (degrees)	Approximate Locations
15–25	15–25	Mexico
26	27	Lower Florida, South Texas
27	29	
28	31	Middle Florida
29	33	
30	35	Middle Texas
31	37	
32	39	Louisiana, Alabama, Georgia
33	41	
34	43	New Mexico, South Carolina
35	45	Arizona, Arkansas, North Carolina
36	47	
37	49	California, Tennessee
38	51	Kansas, Kentucky, Virginia
39	53	Nevada, Colorado, Illinois
40	55	Utah, Ohio, New Jersey
41	57	Pennsylvania
42	59	Nebraska, Iowa
43	61	Wyoming, Connecticut, Rhode Island
44	63	Oregon, Idaho, South Dakota
45	65	Wisconsin, Michigan, New York
Above 45 degrees latitude, add 20 degrees		Washington, Montana, North Dakota, Maine, Alaska, Canada

1. These latitudes run approximately across the middle of the listed states or areas. Although the listed angles of tilt are within 2 degrees of accuracy, panels adjusted to within 4 or 5 degrees are satisfactory. If your state or area is not listed, use the angle of tilt for a neighboring state on or near your latitude.

Installation

Once your planning is complete, assemble your tools and supplies. The panel dealer can provide you with the wire, caulking, mounting brackets, fasteners, and other hardware you will need. Begin by getting your wiring in order:

1. Measure the wire length carefully, from the solar panels down to the controller and then to the battery bank. Allow for plenty of extra wire; add about 25% more than you measure.

2. Using the length measurement from step 1, consult a voltage drop table to determine the wire size you will need (see Table 10-2). You should aim for no more than a 1% voltage drop (0.15 volt). Most installations use either 10- or

8-gauge wire. Also you should use 10/2 or 8/2 wire—i.e., two wires in one sheaf—so you have both the positive and negative wires together. Use multistranded copper automotive or marine-grade wire. *Do not* use Romex solid wire, as it can fracture from vibration, and is unsafe for 12-volt use. The best but most expensive wire is tray cable, which is UV resistant.

3. Cut two lengths—one for the positive wire and one for the negative. They may not be the same length. You may only find wire in 50-foot lengths of single wire, so you will still need the total length from step 1.

4. Establish the route for the wire from the controller to the batteries.

5. Install the wiring harness to the panels before mounting them. Make sure all the wire connections are tight. Give them a good yank so you know the terminals won't come apart. If you use crimp-on connecters, crimp them hard. Or even better, use glue-filled crimp-on connectors.

Now you're ready to mount the panels. If you plan to tilt your panels, make sure your brackets allow tilting. Note: You must securely mount your panels so they won't blow off as you go down the road at 55 or more miles per hour. If a panel gets loose and hits a car or truck behind you, not only could it do a lot of damage, but people could get hurt.

1. If the RV roof has a smooth fiberglass or aluminum skin:
   a. Use 3M VHB Acrylic Foam Tape 4950 to attach brackets to the roof. This tape is not like other mounting tapes; it has a super adhesive on both sides that really holds. A big advantage to using this tape is that you don't have to drill holes in the roof.
   b. The roof must be smooth and clean for the tape to stick. Clean both the roof and the brackets with rubbing alcohol or acetone to remove all traces of grease, oil, or wax.
   c. Install the brackets on the panels.
   d. Put the tape on the brackets and set the whole unit on the roof and press down hard.

2. If the RV roof is rubber or has a fiberglass skin that is not smooth, you will have to drill holes and use screws:
   a. Measure and mark the location of your drill holes. Make the holes slightly smaller than pilot holes you would drill for other work. This is necessary because the rubber usually is fastened to the roof at the edges but only glued to the plywood or composition material. Some of this material will not hold screws very well if the drill hole is too big.
   b. Install the brackets, and set the panels in place.
   c. Drill the holes, then coat the screw ends with a sealant (such as those from Dicor, www.dicor.com) that is specifically designed for rubber

roofs. Do not use a silicone-based caulk on a rubber roof as there is a chemical incompatibility!

    d. After the brackets are screwed down, flow-coat them with Dicor sealant to eliminate any air pockets that might result in leaks.

        At this point, for safety's sake, cover the panels with an old blanket or pieces of cardboard, as the panels are now producing current, and the wiring will be hot.

    e. Secure all the wiring to the roof with ties that have a flat end with a hole so they can be screwed down.

3. If you are installing two panels, now is the time to wire the two panels together in parallel: connect positive post to positive post and negative post to negative post (just as in parallel wiring in Chapter 8).

    If you are installing four or more panels, you must use a combiner box since the system may produce more than 15 amps, which is the rating of the panels' terminals. A combiner box uses heavy-duty metal bus bars that will handle up to 4-gauge wire and will withstand the higher amperage. It can be mounted on the roof next to the panels for convenient wiring.

Once you've mounted the panels, you can continue with your wiring. If you are using a vent pipe or refrigerator vent to route the wiring:

1. Drill and saw an opening where the vent pipe is located in the wall for the controller.

2. Drill a $\frac{1}{2}$-inch hole in the vent pipe.

3. Using a snake, thread the wire down the pipe to the hole, pull the wires through, and strip them.

4. Attach the wires to their respective terminals on the controller.

5. Route the wires down through the wall and to the batteries, which may be through a compartment. Use wire ties to secure the wires and keep them from hanging loose. If the wire must go through the floor of the RV, you may have to cut a hole in the wall next to the floor so you can drill a hole in the floor. You can cover a hole in the wall with an inspection port cover later.

6. Install an appropriately sized fuse on the positive wire within 18 inches of the battery. There are blade-type in-line fuses available but they are not always reliable. A circuit breaker is better.

7. Once the wiring is done, adjust the controller as needed.

8. Some controller models have a temperature compensation feature. If you have one, you will have to run a separate line to the batteries. A separate battery voltage line also may have to be wired.

WIND GENERATORS

Another source of RV battery charging that has not had much publicity in the past is wind generators. Being sailors who lived aboard a sailboat for twelve years, we're familiar with wind generators because they have long been used on sailboats.

In the early 1970s, the only conventional way to charge batteries was to run the propulsion engine and hope the alternator would get the job done—a noisy and expensive way to charge batteries. Solar panels at the time were very expensive and didn't have much amperage output. Their acceptance by the boating community was minimal; consequently, home-built wind generators came into popularity. Some sailors attached old aircraft propellers to automobile alternators, which let them charge their batteries while they were at anchor—the marine equivalent of boondocking.

These early homemade wind generators had many problems, the biggest of which was shutting one off when the wind became too strong without losing an arm or your head. Usually the spinning propeller cut a circle of about 6 feet in diameter, and the generator was mounted in the rigging or on a pole that was mounted on the stern of the boat. The usual procedure was to lock the generator to keep it from weathercocking into the wind, and then either turn the boat or the generator so the propeller was spinning sideways (90 degrees) to the wind. This made the propeller stall. It wasn't as simple as turning off a switch, but it worked. Nowadays, wind generators have smaller propellers (about 45 inches in diameter) with flexible blades that stall out automatically in high winds, thus eliminating the need for removing or disengaging the generator.

Boondocking with a Wind Generator

Are wind generators practical for RV use? It all depends on where you will be boondocking. Some areas of the country are consistently windier than others; e.g., the desert areas of the Southwest. And some topographical areas are better than others. Mountain ridges, coastlines, lakeshores, and hilly areas will be windier than gullies, woods, or the leeward side of a hill. Like solar power, wind energy varies with the season. Unlike solar power, wind energy is more prominent in the winter rather than the summer. So if you boondock year-round, coupling wind and solar power may be a good idea.

An Air-X wind generator. (Southwest Windpower)

But in locations where there are many calm days, wind generators would be of little value. In general, they do not start producing electricity until the wind is blowing at about 7.5 mph and then only produce about 0.2 amp. At 15 mph, they can deliver 2 amps, and at 30 mph, about 11 amps.

Wind generators have similar advantages to solar power:

- Clean and safe: since there is no combustible fuel, there is no fuel to clean up and there are no risks of fire or carbon monoxide poisoning.

- Easy: there are few moving parts.

- Efficient: in contrast to solar power, wind power is available day and night and on cloudy days, too.

The primary disadvantage of course is that wind is fluky. Breezes come and go, and as wind speed changes, so does electrical output. But here again, coupled with other sources of battery charging, a wind generator can be handy to have around.

A Selected List of Boondock Campgrounds

Since there are so many places to boondock in the United States, we won't attempt to list every possible campsite. Our goal is to list camping areas in nearly every state that we know personally or have heard about from friends.

Generally, western states have the most places to boondock, while the more densely populated states, where more of the land is privately owned, have fewer. And most of these more populated states have laws and regulations prohibiting random camping along highways.

Many states in the Northeast have numerous full-service RV parks but only a few primitive areas. This doesn't mean boondocking places don't exist; they just may be harder to find and farther apart, and they may have limitations, such as size restrictions or unsuitable approach roads. Chapter 2 discusses boondocking options in much more detail.

Here are just a few reminders when looking for a campsite:

- Explore a campsite before you drive into it in your RV. We have seen too many parks that looked or sounded great, but had undesirable or risky conditions: trees down, roads washed out, and trees and bushes growing in the sites or on the road. These all create hazards for your RV.

- Watch for steep grades. One problem with eastern states such as Virginia, North Carolina, and Georgia is the mountain roads, and particularly those going up to the Blue Ridge Parkway. The roads leading to many of the campgrounds in those states can have grades from 7% to 10%—much steeper than most roads in the West. So be careful. We recommend avoiding steep grades. If you use common sense, you will probably be all right.

- Remember that campgrounds vary and can change over time. Options offered by campgrounds—such as hookups, water, and RV length accommodated—can change from year to year. We've found many wonderful used-to-be boondocking areas that now have electricity, water and sewer hookups . . . and charge a good deal more money today than we paid in the past. It's always a good idea to research an area before you go.

■ Find your own favorite campsites. This is one of the most enjoyable things about boondock camping. As you travel, visit every likely place you come across, make notes for future reference, and mark their locations on a map. Some of the very best places are those that are the farthest from civilization.

CAMPGROUNDS AND SITES BY STATE

Alabama

Wilson Dam—Lower Rockpile Campground (TVA), Muscle Shoals. Description: fee, 23 sites. Directions: SR-133 0.5 mile west from south side of dam, then 0.5 mile north and follow the signs. Contact: 256-386-2231; www.tva.gov/river/recreation/camping.htm#wilson.

Gunter Hill Campground (USACE), Montgomery. Description: fee, 146 sites, dump station. Directions: US-80 west 9 miles from Montgomery, turn right on CR-7, then follow the signs. Contact: 334-269-1053; http://al-lakes.sam.usace.army.mil/gunter_hill_campground.htm.

Alaska

The whole state of Alaska is practically one big boondock campground. You do need to get permission from owners of private property before camping. Dry camping is allowed in many places including grocery and drugstore parking lots. Some Wal-Marts and Kmarts allow parking overnight, but always check with store managers first. Below are a few campgrounds that we think are "must stops."

Denali State Park. Description: 4 campgrounds, 123 sites, toilets, water. Directions: 163 miles north of Anchorage next to Denali National Park. Contact: 907-269-8400; www.dnr.state.ak.us/parks/units/denali2.htm.

Denali National Park and Preserve is one place in Alaska where you should spend several days; the scenery is spectacular, and you will see more wildlife there in just a few hours than in other places in several days. It has three campgrounds that accommodate RVs:

Savage River Campground. Description: fee, 33 sites, toilets, water. Directions: Mile 13 on the Park Road. Contact: 1-800-622-7275; www.nps.gov/dena/planyourvisit/campground-reservations.htm.

Riley Creek Campground. Description: fee, 150 sites, toilets, water. Directions: just inside park entrance. Contact: 1-800-622-7275; www.nps.gov/dena/planyourvisit/campground-reservations.htm.

Teklanika River Campground. Description: fee, 53 sites, toilets, water. Directions: Mile 29 on the Park Road. Contact: 1-800-622-7275; www.nps.gov/dena/planyourvisit/campground-reservations.htm.

Arizona

Arizona is one of the most popular states for boondock camping, so this is only a sampling of the many sites available.

Quartzsite is considered the boondocking mecca. From January to March, the population of this little town swells from 2,000 to about 500,000. For many miles south along US-95, you will see RV after RV boondocking on the desert. You need a permit to boondock. Short-term permits are good for up to fourteen days; long-term permits are valid for up to seven months. You can obtain one at the La Posa Long-Term Visitor Area or the BLM Yuma Field Office. Contact: 928-317-3200; www.blm.gov/az/outrec/camping/laposa.htm.

Mather Campground, Grand Canyon National Park. Description: fee, 319 sites, dump station. Directions: I-40 to SR-64N, 0.5 mile south of town. Contact: 1-877-444-6777; www.nps.gov/grca/planyourvisit/cg-sr.htm.

Lees Ferry Campground, Glen Canyon National Recreation Area. Description: fee, 55 sites, dump station. Directions: US-89A 5 miles north of Marble Canyon. Contact: 928-608-6200; www.nps.gov/glca/planyourvisit/lees-ferry.htm.

Lost Dutchman State Park. Description: fee, 35 sites, dump station. Directions: SR-88 5 miles north of Apache Junction. Contact: 480-982-4485; www.azparks.gov/Parks/parkhtml/dutchman.html.

Picacho Peak State Park. Description: fee, 25 sites (some with water and electric), dump station. Directions: I-10 40 miles north of Tucson. Contact: 520-466-3183; www.azparks.gov/Parks/parkhtml/picacho.html.

Burro Creek Recreation Site. Description: fee, 24 sites, dump station. Directions: I-40 17 miles east of Kingman, then US-93 54 miles south to Burro Creek Bridge. Contact: 928-718-3700; www.blm.gov/az/outrec/camping/burrocr.htm.

Arkansas

Most of the primitive campgrounds in Arkansas are National Park Service sites.

Buffalo National River. Description: fee, 10+ campgrounds (all but one—Lost Valley—along the river), water, toilets. Directions: Upper District—SR-7 or SR-43 south from Harrison; Middle District—SR-65 31 miles south of Harrison; Lower District—SR-65 5 miles south from Harrison, then SR-62/412 east to Yellville, and SR-14 south. Contact: 1-877-444-6777; www.nps.gov/buff/planyourvisit/feesandreservations.htm.

Gulpha Gorge Campground, Hot Springs National Park. Description: fee, 43 sites, water, toilets, dump station. Directions: located in downtown Hot Springs. Contact: 501-620-6715; www.nps.gov/hosp/planyourvisit/campground.htm.

California

California has too many boondocking sites to list; we've included just a few that we know about or that have been recommended to us.

Yosemite National Park. There are so many sites that your best bet is to visit the website and browse all the choices. An alternative we recommend is driving in as a side trip, especially in the summer. Contact: 209-372-0200; www.nps.gov/yose/planyourvisit/campground.htm.

Sequoia and Kings Canyon National Parks. Description: fee, 10 campgrounds for RVs, most have flush toilets and water. Contact: 1-877-444-6777; www.nps.gov/seki/planyourvisit/campgrounds.htm.

Death Valley National Park offers beautiful desert scenery and mountain views. Description: fee (some are free), 6 campgrounds that accommodate RVs, water, flush or pit toilets, dump station (some). Contact: 760-786-3200; www.nps.gov/deva/planyourvisit/camping.htm.

Emma Wood State Beach. Description: fee, 90 sites. Directions: SR-101 2 miles west of Ventura. Contact: 805-968-1033; www.parks.ca.gov/default.asp?page_id=604.

McGrath State Beach. Description: 174 sites, water, dump station. Directions: SR-101 via Harbor Boulevard 5 miles south of Ventura. Contact: 805-968-1033; www.parks.ca.gov/default.asp?page_id=607.

Colorado

Colorado is high on the list of states popular with RVers, with several national parks that attract many tourists and offer good primitive camping.

One of our favorites is **Rocky Mountain National Park**. Early in our marriage, all of our vacations were spent there. It has 4 RV campgrounds; all charge a fee: **Aspenglen:** 54 sites, no facilities; **Glacier Basin:** 150 sites, flush toilets, dump station; **Moraine Park:** 245 sites, water when available, flush toilets, dump station; **Timber Creek:** 98 sites, water when available, flush toilets, dump station. Contact: 1-888-448-1474; www.nps.gov/romo/planyourvisit/camping.htm.

Difficult Campground, White River National Forest. Description: fee, 47 sites, water, vault toilets, dump station. Directions: SR-82 5 miles southeast of Aspen. Contact: 970-925-3445; www.fs.fed.us/r2/whiteriver/recreation/campgrounds/aspencg/difficultcg.

Connecticut

Rocky Neck State Park. Description: fee, 160 sites, showers, dump station. Directions: I-95 (Exit 72), turnpike connector south to SR-156, turn left and take SR-156 east for 0.25 mile. Contact: 860-739-5471; www.ct.gov/dep/cwp/view.asp?a=2716&q=325258&depNav_GID=1621.

Delaware

Cape Henlopen State Park is a great place to be on a hot day. Description: fee, 139 sites with water, 17 with no facilities, showers, dump station. Directions: 1 mile east of Lewes. Contact: 302-645-2103; www.destateparks.com/chsp/fishcamp.asp.

Florida

Because of Florida's popularity as a winter vacation spot, there are probably more RV parks and campgrounds per square mile there than in any other state. Florida is not great boondocking territory, though, but we found a few places around the **Everglades National Park** with primitive campsites:

Flamingo Campground. Description: fee, 234 sites (55 with a water view), showers, dump station. Directions: SR-9336 southwest from Florida City to the end of the main park road. Contact: 1-800-365-CAMP; www.nps.gov/ever/planyourvisit/flamcamp.htm.

Long Pine Key Campground. Description: fee, 108 sites, water, dump station. Directions: SR-9336 southwest from Florida City to Long Pine Key entrance. Contact: 305-242-7873; www.nps.gov/ever/planyourvisit/longpinecamp.htm.

Big Cypress National Preserve. Description: 4 small campgrounds along the Tamiami Trail (US-41) don't charge a fee. Contact: 239-695-1201; www.nps.gov/bicy/planyourvisit/campgrounds.htm.

Casinos. There are three Indian casinos in the Miami area that allow overnight parking, but you must check with security before parking. **Seminole Coconut Creek Casino** (www.seminolecoconutcreekcasino.com); Directions: I-95 (Exit 39), 4.5 miles west on Sample Road to NW 54th Street, then right 0.5 mile. **Seminole Hollywood Casino** (www.seminolehollywoodcasino.com); Directions: I-95 (Exit 22) to Stirling Road, then west to SR-7 (US-441). **Miccosukee Indian Gaming Casino, Miami** (www.miccosukee.com); Directions: Florida Turnpike Homestead Extension (Exit 25), then US-41 5.7 miles west. In Immokalee, north and west of Miami, there is the **Seminole Casino** (www.theseminolecasino.com); Directions: I-75 to SR-29 north, then 35 miles east on SR-846.

Georgia

Georgia has many state parks (www.gastateparks.org), but they all have full hookups and no primitive camping. There are a few primitive campgrounds near the Blue Ridge Area, but they are on steep and winding roads and may not be accessible for big rigs.

Idaho

Idaho is a state with many boondocking possibilities.

City of Rocks National Reserve is a famous California Trail site and one of our favorite camps. The granite rock towers are beautiful. Description: fee, 64 sites, water (from the pump well along Emery Canyon Road), vault toilets. Directions: SR-77 50 miles south of Burley to Almo, then 2 miles west of Almo. Contact: 208-824-5519; www.nps.gov/ciro/planyourvisit/feesandreservations.htm.

Lava Flow Campground, Craters of the Moon National Monument and Preserve, is a fascinating area of former volcanic activity. Description: fee, 51 sites, flush toilets, grills, tables. Directions: From junction of US-26 and US-20, go southwest 18 miles on US-20 to entrance. Contact: 208-527-3257; www.nps.gov/crmo/planyourvisit/campground.htm.

Holman Creek Campground, Sawtooth National Forest, is another of our favorite camps. Description: fee, 10 sites, pit toilets. Directions: SR-75 7 miles east of Clayton. Contact: 208-774-3000; www.publiclands.org/explore/site.php?search=YES&back=Search%20Results&id=2557.

Illinois

Des Plaines Fish and Wildlife Area. Description: 24 sites, water, pit toilets, dump station. Directions: I-55 (Wilmington exit), 10 miles south on North River Road. Contact: 815-423-5326; http://dnr.state.il.us/lands/Landmgt/PARKS/i&m/EAST/DESPLAIN/PARK.htm.

Johnson-Sauk Trail State Park. Description: 89 sites, flush toilets, dump station. Directions: SR-78 5 miles north of Kewanee. Contact: 309-853-5589; http://dnr.state.il.us/lands/Landmgt/PARKS/R1/JOHNSON.htm.

Iowa

Harrah's Council Bluffs Casino. Directions: I-29 (9th Avenue exit), turn right, park in the north lot, and check with security. Contact: 712-329-6000; www.harrahs.com/casinos/harrahs-council-bluffs/hotel-casino/property-home.shtml.

Ameristar Casino Council Bluffs. Directions: I-29 (Exit 52), follow the truck parking signs to the south lot. Contact: www.ameristar.com/council.

Iowa has lots of state parks with campgrounds. Most of the parks have electric hookups, but almost every park has some sites that are primitive. For more information, go to www.iowadnr.com/parks/camping/general_info.html.

Kansas

Almost all of Kansas's state parks offer utility and primitive camping. For more information, go to www.kdwp.state.ks.us/news/state_parks/about_state_parks.

Louisiana

Fontainebleau State Park. Description: fee, 37 primitive sites (plus more sites with hookups). Directions: I-12 to US-190 toward Mandeville, then follow signs. Contact: 985-624-4443; www.crt.state.la.us/parks/iFontaine.aspx. **Note:** This park was affected by Hurricane Katrina; check the website for the latest updates.

Maine

Maine has 11 state parks (www.maine.gov/doc/parks/programs) with primitive camping. We particularly recommend the following two state parks.

Aroostook State Park. Description: fee, 30 sites, showers, dump station. Directions: west off US-1, south of Presque Isle. Contact: 207-768-8341.

Lamoine State Park. Description: 61 sites, flush toilets, showers. Directions: SR-184 off US-1A 8 miles. Contact: 207-667-4778.

Blackwoods Campground, Acadia National Park. Description: fee, 306 sites (some accessible), restrooms, water, dump station. Directions: SR-3 5 miles south of Bar Harbor. Contact: 207-288-3388; www.nps.gov/acad/planyourvisit/blackwoodscampground.htm.

Seawall Campground, Acadia National Park. Description: fee, 214 sites (some accessible), restrooms, water, dump station. Directions: SR-102A 4 miles south of Southwest Harbor. Contact: 207-288-3388; www.nps.gov/acad/planyourvisit/seawallcampground.htm.

Maryland

Greenbelt Park Campground, National Capital Parks East. Description: 174 sites, showers, restrooms, dump stations. Directions: I-95 (Exit 23), left on SR-193 (Greenbelt Road), 0.25 mile to park. Contact: 1-800-365-2267; www.nps.gov/gree/planyourvisit/campground.htm.

Massachusetts

Nickerson State Park. Description: 420 sites, showers, dump station. Directions: US-6A from Orleans west toward Brewster 2 miles. Contact: 508-896-3491; www.mass.gov/dcr/parks/southeast/nick.htm.

Wells State Park. Description: 60 sites, showers, dump station. Directions: I-90 (Exit 9) to US-20, east for 2 miles to SR-49 North, then third left. Contact: 508-347-9257; www.mass.gov/dcr/parks/central/well.htm.

Michigan

Michigan has a few parks with primitive sites. For more information, go to www.michigandnr.com/parksandtrails.

Minnesota

Gooseberry Falls State Park. Description: 70 sites (large, some pull-throughs), dump station. Directions: SR-61 13 miles northeast of Two Harbors. Contact: 218-834-3855; www.dnr.state.mn.us/ state_parks/gooseberry_falls.

Mississippi

The **Natchez Trace Parkway** area is beautiful, especially in the fall. Two campgrounds there we like are:

Jeff Busby Campground. Description: 18 sites, no facilities. Directions: milepost 193.1 on the Natchez Trace Parkway. Contact: 1-800-305-7417; www.nps.gov/natr/camping.htm.

Rocky Springs Campground. Description: 22 sites, no facilities. Directions: milepost 54.8 on the Natchez Trace Parkway. Contact: 1-800-305-7417; www.nps.gov/natr/camping.htm.

Missouri

Arrow Rock State Historic Site preserves the history of this river town that was a stop at the beginning of the Sante Fe Trail. Description: 12 basic sites, showers, water, dump station.

Directions: I-70 (Exit 98) to SR-41, then 13 miles north. Contact: 660-837-3330; www.mostateparks.com/arrowrock/camp.htm.

Table Rock State Park. Description: 43 basic sites, restrooms, showers, water, dump station. Directions: off SR-165 7 miles southwest of Branson. Reservations required. Contact: 417-334-4704; www.mostateparks.com/tablerock/camp.htm.

Montana

Montana's state parks all offer primitive camping. Plus, many city and county parks offer boondock camping. See also page 22 in Chapter 2 for two areas we enjoy boondocking in.

Medicine Rocks State Park is a favorite of ours. The rock formations are fascinating, and it has beautiful sunsets. Description: 22 sites, no facilities. Directions: SR-7 25 miles south of Baker. Contact: 406-234-0900; http://fwp.mt.gov/lands/site_283951.aspx.

Glacier National Park is probably the most beautiful park in the country. Description: fee, 7 campgrounds accommodate RVs, restrooms, water. Directions: US-2 from the east or west; US-89 or US-17 from the north. Contact: 406-888-7800; www.nps.gov/glac/planyourvisit/camping.htm. **Note:** The Going-to-the-Sun Road has some vehicle size restrictions, but shuttles are available.

Nebraska

Nebraska, our birth state, is one that some people call a "flyover" state but there is a lot of history here—the Oregon Trail, the Pony Express, the transcontinental railroad, Crazy Horse, and Buffalo Bill. Plus, it has plenty of places to boondock.

Most of Nebraska's state parks have a small number of primitive sites where you can boondock if you wish. For more information, go to www.ngpc.state.ne.us/parks.

One of our favorite parks is **Rock Creek Station State Recreation Area**. Description: fee, 10 primitive sites, restrooms, showers, dump station. Directions: PWF road 4.5 miles east from Fairbury, 573 Avenue 1 mile south, 710 Road 1.25 miles east. Contact: 402-729-5777; www.ngpc.state.ne.us/parks/guides/parksearch/showpark.asp?Area_No=150.

Nevada

Nevada is a good dry camping state, with many places to stay.

Thomas Canyon Campground, Lamoille Canyon, Humboldt-Toiyabe National Forest. As we described in Chapter 2 (see page 21), this is one of our all-time favorite places. Description: 39 sites, drinking water, pit toilets. Directions: SR-227 south from Elko to Lamoille Canyon Road. Contact: 775-752-3357; www.fs.fed.us/r4/htnf/recreation/camp_picnic/rubymts_camp/thomas_canyon_campground.shtml.

Valley of Fire State Park has beautiful red rock formations. This was the first place we tried boondocking back in 1982. Description: fee, 51 sites, showers, water, dump station. Directions: I-15 to SR-169. Contact: 702-397-2088; http://parks.nv.gov/vf.htm.

New Mexico

El Morro National Monument. Description: fee, 9 sites, water, pit toilets. Directions: I-40 from Albuquerque to Grants, then SR-53 42 miles south. Contact: 505-783-4226; www.nps.gov/elmo/planyourvisit/campgrounds.htm.

El Malpais National Monument is an interesting volcanic area. Note that some roads have sharp curves that can be a problem for large RVs. Description: some primitive camping available—check at the Information Center. Directions: SR-53 23 miles south of Grants. Contact: 505-783-4774; www.nps.gov/elma/planyourvisit/index.htm.

New York

New York State has over 100 state parks; most have electric hookups, but there are some primitive parks.

Beaver Pond Campgrounds, Harriman State Park. Description: 146 sites, restrooms, showers, dump station. Directions: Palisades Parkway to Lake Welch Parkway. Contact: 845-947-2792; http://nysparks.state.ny.us/parks/info.asp?parkID=57.

North Carolina

Cape Hatteras National Seashore has four campgrounds. Contact: 252-473-2111; www.nps.gov/caha/planyourvisit/campgrounds.htm:

Cape Point Campground. Description: fee, 202 sites, water, showers, toilets, dump station. Directions: NC-12 near Cape Hatteras Light, 2 miles south of Buxton.

Frisco Campground. Description: fee, 127 sites, water, showers, toilets. Directions: NC-12, east of Frisco and southwest of Buxton.

Ocracoke Campground. Description: fee, 136 sites, water, showers, toilets, dump station. Directions: NC-12, east of Ocracoke.

Oregon Inlet Campground. Description: fee, 120 sites, water, showers, toilets, dump stations. Directions: NC-12, 9 miles south of Whalebone Junction.

North Dakota

Theodore Roosevelt National Park has two campgrounds that accommodate RVs:

Cottonwood Campground, South Unit. Description: fee, 76 sites, flush toilets, water. Directions: I-94 (exits 23 and 27), 5 miles from park entrance near Medora. Contact: 701-623-4466; www.nps.gov/thro/planyourvisit/cottonwood-campground.htm.

Juniper Campground, North Unit. Description: fee, 50 sites, flush toilets, water, dump station. Directions: US-85 16 miles south of Watford City. Contact: 701-842-2233; www.nps.gov/thro/planyourvisit/juniper-campground.htm.

Ohio

Almost all of Ohio's state parks have some primitive sites. For more information, go to www.dnr.state.oh.us/parks.

Oklahoma

This state is gambler's heaven with 26 casinos all over the state. They all seem to allow overnight camping if you gamble and patronize the facilities. Please check with security before parking, and remember the rules of camping on others' property: no awnings, no chairs, and no slideouts until evening.

Oregon

Oregon has more than 50 state parks with year-round and seasonal campgrounds; we list some of our favorites below. The **Willamette National Forest** has lots of boondocking possibilities; for more information, go to www.fs.fed.us/r6/willamette/recreation/camping. Oregon also has several casinos in the western part of the state.

Cape Lookout State Park. Description: fee, 38 full-hookup sites, 1 site with electrical hookup, 173 tent sites, restrooms, water, showers, dump station. Directions: US-101 12 miles southwest of Tillamook. Contact: www.oregonstateparks.org/park_186.php.

Farewell Bend State Recreation Area. Description: fee, 101 sites with electrical hookups, 30 tent sites, showers, dump station. Directions: I-84 (Exit 353), then 1 mile north. Contact: 541-869-2365; www.oregonstateparks.org/park_7.php.

South Beach State Park. Description: fee, 228 sites with electrical hookups, restrooms, water, showers, dump station. Directions: US-101 2 miles south of Newport. Contact: 541-867-4715; www.oregonstateparks.org/park_209.php.

Pennsylvania

Go to www.dcnr.state.pa.us/stateparks for more information on Pennsylvania's state parks.

Rhode Island

Burlingame State Campground, Burlingame State Park. Description: fee, 755 sites, restrooms, showers, water, dump stations. Directions: US-1 south to Charlestown. Contact: 401-322-7337; www.riparks.com/burlgmcamp.htm.

South Dakota

South Dakota has many boondocking campsites, particularly in the Black Hills.

Custer State Park. Description: fee, 11 camping areas (23 to 71 sites each, all primitive sites), showers, restrooms, water. Directions: near Mount Rushmore at junction of US-16 and SR-385. Contact: 605-255-4515; www.sdgfp.info/Parks/Regions/Custer/index.htm.

The Slim Buttes area in **Custer National Forest** is an old favorite of ours. The U.S. Cavalry fought the Sioux here and won—its first significant victory after Custer's defeat at Little Bighorn. The buttes are beautiful.

Reva Gap Campground, Sioux Ranger District, Custer National Forest. Description: 4 sites. Directions: SR-20 20 miles east of Buffalo, just west of Reva. Contact: 605-797-4432; www.fs.fed.us/r1/custer/recreation/campgrounds.shtml.

Badlands National Park has two campgrounds. Contact: 605-433-5361; www.nps.gov/badl:

Cedar Pass Campground. Description: fee, 96 sites, toilets, dump station. Directions: I-90 (Exit 131), then 8 miles south to SR-240.

Sage Creek Campground. Description: fee, 15 sites, pit toilets. Directions: 30 miles northwest of visitor center on SD-240 and Sage Creek Rim Road. A high-clearance vehicle is required to travel on Sage Creek Rim Road.

Texas

The state of Texas has so many good places to boondock, you could spend years camping in different locations. Two places we like a lot are the hill country around Fredericksburg and the area around Fort Davis. There are also many places to camp along the Guadalupe River. In addition, we recommend camping in two national parks:

Cottonwood Campground, Big Bend National Park. Description: fee, 31 sites, pit toilets, water. Directions: 22 miles south of Santa Elena Junction off Ross Maxwell Scenic Drive. Contact: 432-477-2251; www.nps.gov/bibe/planyourvisit/cottonwood_campground.htm.

Rio Grande Village Campground, Big Bend National Park. Description: fee, 100 sites, flush toilets, water, dump station nearby. Directions: 20 miles southeast of Panther Junction. Contact: 432-477-2251; www.nps.gov/bibe/planyourvisit/rgv_campground.htm.

Padre Island National Seashore is almost the perfect wintertime boondocking camp site, like Quartzsite. It has four campgrounds that accommodate RVs. Directions: SR-358 east from Corpus Christi to Padre Island, then 10 miles south on Park Road 22. Contact: 361-949-8068; www.nps.gov/pais/planyourvisit/camping.htm.

Bird Island Basin. Description: fee, no designated sites, chemical toilets.

Malaquite. Description: fee, 42 RV sites, toilets, rinse showers, water and dump station nearby.

North Beach. Description: no designated sites, no facilities.

South Beach. Description: no designated sites, no facilities. RVers park their vehicles in the first 5 miles of beach from the end of Park Road.

Utah

Utah has a number of beautiful national parks. We have visited all of them, and enjoy going back again and again. We like Arches, Bryce, Canyonlands, and Capitol Reef the best.

Devils Garden Campground, Arches National Park. Description: fee, 52 sites, toilets, water. Directions: US-191 5 miles north of Moab. Contact: 435-719-2299; www.nps.gov/arch/planyourvisit/camping.htm.

North Campground, Bryce Canyon National Park. Description: fee, 107 sites, restrooms, water. Directions: opposite vistor center, which is 4.5 miles south of intersection of UT-12 and UT-63. Contact: 435-834-5322; www.nps.gov/brca/planyourvisit/northcampground.htm.

Sunset Campground, Bryce Canyon National Park. Description: fee, 50 sites, restrooms, water. Directions: 2 miles south of vistor center, which is 4.5 miles south of intersection of UT-12 and UT-63. Contact: 435-834-5322; www.nps.gov/brca/planyourvisit/sunsetcampground.htm.

Squaw Flat Campground, Canyonlands National Park. Description: fee, 26 sites, restrooms, water. Directions: US-191 south from Moab to SR-211, then 35 miles to visitor center, then west. Contact: 435-719-2313; www.nps.gov/cany/planyourvisit/camping.htm.

Willow Flat Campground, Canyonlands National Park. Description: fee, 12 sites, vault toilets. Directions: US-191 north from Moab to SR-313, then 22 miles to visitor center, then 6 miles south. Contact: 435-719-2313; www.nps.gov/cany/planyourvisit/camping.htm.

Fruita Campground, Capitol Reef National Park. Description: fee, 71 sites, restrooms, water, dump station. Directions: SR-24 to visitor center, then 1 mile south. Contact: 435-425-3791; www.nps.gov/care/planyourvisit/fruitacampground.htm.

Vermont

None of Vermont's state parks have hookups, so they're great for boondocking. For more information, go to www.vtstateparks.com.

Virginia

Virginia has some great locations—such as the Chesapeake Bay—but not many primitive campgrounds. There are places in the Blue Ridge Parkway area, but we hesitate to recommend them because of the winding, steep roads in the mountains. It's best to scout where you want to go by car or pickup truck first. For more information, go to www.dcr.virginia.gov/state_parks.

Washington

Washington's state parks have a lot to offer, including primitive camping. For more information, go to www.parks.wa.gov/parks. We've also boondocked in the following locations:

Two Rivers Casino RV Park. Description: fee, 100 full-hookup sites but overnight parking allowed in parking lot (contact security first). Directions: SR-25 20 miles north of Davenport. Contact: 509-722-4029; www.tworiverscasinoandresort.com.

Lake Roosevelt National Recreation Area has 27 campgrounds. Most accommodate RVs (without hookups) but some are only reachable by boat. Contact: 509-633-9441; www.nps.gov/laro/planyourvisit/campgrounds.htm.

Mount Rainier National Park has five campgrounds suitable for RVs. The park experienced severe flooding in 2006, so you should check ahead of time to see what roads and campgrounds are open. As of this writing, only Cougar Rock, Ohanapecosh, and White River campgrounds will be open in 2007. Contact: 360-569-2211; www.nps.gov/mora/planyourvisit/camping.htm.

Wyoming

Wyoming is a wonderful state for boondocking. We have done primitive camping all over the state. All BLM land is usually open for camping. In addition to the places we mentioned on pages 21–22 in Chapter 2, we have camped in the city parks in Douglas and Sheridan and along Sinks Canyon Road between Lander and SR-28.

One of our all-time favorite spots is **Grand Teton National Park**, which has several campgrounds that accommodate RVs:

Colter Bay Campground. Description: fee, 350 sites, flush toilets, showers, dump stations. Directions: 25 miles north of Moose Visitor Center, which is 12 miles north of Jackson. Contact: 1-800-628-9988; www.nps.gov/grte/planyourvisit/campgrounds.htm.

Gros Ventre Campground. Description: fee, 360 sites, dump station. Directions: 11.5 miles south and east of Moose Visitor Center, which is 12 miles north of Jackson. Contact: 1-800-628-9988; www.nps.gov/grte/planyourvisit/campgrounds.htm.

Lizard Creek Campground. Description: fee, 60 sites. Directions: 32 miles north of Moose Visitor Center, which is 12 miles north of Jackson. Contact: 1-800-672-6012; www.nps.gov/grte/planyourvisit/campgrounds.htm.

Signal Mountain Campground. Description: fee, 81 sites, dump station. Directions: 16 miles north of Jenny Lake Visitor Center, which is 8 miles north of the Moose Visitor Center. Contact: 1-800-672-6012; www.nps.gov/grte/planyourvisit/campgrounds.htm.

Yellowstone National Park. Description: 12 camping areas—some have restaurants, grocery stores, hot showers, boat ramps, and allow generators to be run, in addition to toilets, water, and dump stations. Contact: 307-344-7311; www.nps.gov/yell/planyourvisit/camping-in-yellowstone.htm. **Note:** Avoid using US-20 and US-212 going into or out of Yellowstone because of long, steep grades.

Wyoming's state parks are also good primitive camping areas. Contact: 800-225-5996; http://wyoparks.state.wy.us.

Resources

AM Solar
P.O. Box 696
Springfield, OR 97477
541-726-1091
Fax: 541-736-1107
www.amsolar.com
Solar panels, charge controllers, and
accessories

Bachman Enterprises
P.O. Box 6159
Gardnerville, NV 89460
800-326-4410; 775-265-3003
www.turbokool.com
TurboKOOL swamp coolers

Barker Manufacturing
730 E. Michigan Avenue
Battle Creek, MI 49016
800-537-9940; 269-965-2371
Fax: 269-965-2389
www.barkermfg.com
Tote-Along gray- and black-water portable
holding tanks

Blue Sky Energy
2598 Fortune Way, Suite K
Vista, CA 92081
800-493-7877; 760-597-1642
Fax: 760-597-1731
www.blueskyenergyinc.com

Camping World
P.O. Box 90017
Bowling Green, KY 42102
800-626-3636
www.campingworld.com
Retail stores and online site with a wide
variety of RV and camping products

Coast Distribution System
350 Woodview Avenue
Morgan Hill, CA 95037
408-782-6686
Fax: 408-782-7790
www.coastdistribution.com
Tote-N-Stor gray- and black-water portable
holding tanks

East Penn Manufacturing Company
Deka Road
Lyon Station, PA 19536
610-682-6361
Fax: 610-682-4781
www.eastpenn-deka.com
Deka batteries

Escapees RV Club
100 Rainbow Drive
Livingston, TX 77351
888-757-2582
Fax: 936-327-4388
www.escapees.com
Offers many services; see the website for
details

Fan-tastic Vent
2083 S. Almont Avenue
Imlay City, MI 48444
800-521-0298; 810-724-3818
Fax: 810-724-3460
www.fantasticvent.com
Vent fans

Heliotrope PV
P.O. Box 696
Springfield, OR 97477
541-726-1091
Fax: 541-736-1107
www.heliotrope-pv.com
Solar charge controllers

Iota Engineering
P.O. Box 11846
Tucson, AZ 85734
520-294-3292
Fax: 520-741-2837
www.iotaengineering.com
Smart battery chargers

Lifeline Batteries
955 Todd Avenue
Azusa, CA 91702
800-527-3224; 626-969-6886
Fax: 626-969-8566
www.lifelinebatteries.com
Lifeline batteries

Magnum Energy
1111 80th Street SW, Suite 250
Everett, WA 98203
425-353-8833
Fax: 425-353-8390
www.magnumenergy.com
Pure-sine-wave inverters

Navimo USA
7455 16th Street East, Suite 107
Sarasota, FL 34243
866-383-1888
Fax: 866-214-1400
www.navimousa.com
Flexible water tanks

Northwood Manufacturing
P.O. Box 3359
La Grande, OR 97850
800-766-6274; 541-962-6274
www.northwoodmfg.com
Nash and Arctic Fox travel trailers

Progressive Dynamics
507 Industrial Road
Marshall, MI 49068
269-781-4241
Fax: 269-781-7802
www.progressivedyn.com
Converter/chargers

Recreational Vehicle Industry Associaton
   (RVIA)
1896 Preston White Drive
Reston, VA 20191
703-620-6003
Fax: 703-620-5071
www.rvia.org
National RV trade association

RV Solar Electric
P.O. Box 25313
Scottsdale, AZ 85255
800-999-8520; 480-443-8520
Fax: 480-443-0742
www.rvsolarelectric.com
Solar systems

Southwest Windpower
1801 W. Route 66
Flagstaff, AZ 86001
928-779-9463
Fax: 928-779-1485
www.windenergy.com
Wind generators

Sun Ovens International
39W835 Midan Drive
Elburn, IL 60119
800-408-7919; 630-208-7273
Fax: 630-208-7386
www.sunoven.com
Global Sun Oven

West Marine
P.O. Box 50070
Watsonville, CA 95077
800-728-2700
www.westmarine.com
Retail stores and online site with a huge
    variety of products

Wrangler NW Power Products
5061 N. Lagoon Avenue
Portland, OR 97217
503-235-4110
Fax: 503-517-0753
www.wranglernw.com
High-powered alternators

Xantrex Technology
800-670-0707
Fax: 360-925-5143
www.xantrex.com
Wide variety of power supply
    products

Recommended Reading

Bannan, Jan. *Great Western RV Trips.* Camden, Maine: Ragged Mountain Press, 1998.

Church, Mike, and Terri Church. *Pacific Northwest Camping Destinations.* Kirkland, Washington: Rolling Homes Press, 2006.

———. *Southwest Camping Destinations.* Kirkland, Washington: Rolling Homes Press, 2006.

———. *Traveler's Guide to Alaskan Camping.* Kirkland, Washington: Rolling Homes Press, 2006.

———. *Traveler's Guide to Camping Mexico's Baja.* Kirkland, Washington: Rolling Homes Press, 2006.

———. *Traveler's Guide to Mexican Camping.* Kirkland, Washington: Rolling Homes Press, 2006.

Davin, D. J. *RV Camping in State Parks.* Lenexa, Kansas: Roundabout Publications, 2007.

Groene, Janet, and Gordon Groene. *Great Eastern RV Trips.* Camden, Maine: Ragged Mountain Press, 2000.

Herow, William C. *National Park Service Camping Guide.* 3rd ed. Lenexa, Kansas: Roundabout Publications, 2007.

Hinkle, Spurgeon L. *Camping with the Corps of Engineers.* 6th ed. Elkhart, Indiana: Cottage Publications, 2005.

Kenny, Jane. *Casino Camping.* Lenexa, Kansas: Roundabout Publications, 2006.

———. *RVer's Guide to Corps of Engineers Campgrounds.* Lenexa, Kansas: Roundabout Publications, 2007.

———. *Rest Areas & Welcome Centers Along US Interstates.* Lenexa, Kansas: Roundabout Publications, 2001.

Moeller, Bill, and Jan Moeller. *RV Electrical Systems.* Camden, Maine: Ragged Mountain Press, 1995.

———. *RVing Basics.* Camden, Maine: Ragged Mountain Press, 1995.

Tisdale, Mary, and Bibi Booth, eds. *Adventures on America's Public Lands.* Washington, D.C.: Smithsonian, 2003.

Index

Numbers in **bold** refer to pages with illustrations